Henry VIII is widely remembered as a fat, corrupt tyrant, feared and hated by his people, who cut off the heads of two of his six wives and cruelly divorced two more. Books, plays and films have shown him as a greedy, bad-tempered king, who spent on idle pleasure the money his father had saved by good government, who in a fit of rage could order the execution of a minister or a friend, and who cut England off from the Catholic Church to gratify a personal whim.

In this book, David Fletcher shows that the popular view of Henry is partly true—a long and painful illness, and the bitterness of his divorce from Catherine of Aragon and the dissolution of the monasteries, turned the king into an unpleasant, capricious old man. But the author also reveals the other side of Henry—the talented young Renaissance prince, the skilled musician and friend of artists and intellectuals, of whom the Dutch scholar Erasmus was told: "Our King is not after gold, or gems, or precious metals, but virtue, glory, immortality." He explains, too, how Henry's two great ministers, Thomas Wolsey and Thomas Cromwell, built up the Tudor system of government which reached its peak under Henry's daughter Elizabeth.

What qualities did the glamorous young hero and the decadent old despot have in common? David Fletcher argues that throughout his life Henry was arrogant and selfish, always placing his own interests and desires above those of his people. The King's close friend Sir Thomas More, later Lord Chancellor, summed up this attitude: "If my head would win a castle in France, it should not fail to go."

With the lavish use of contemporary quotations and illustrations, David Fletcher offers a perceptive portrait of the monarch as man and as statesman at a crucial period in English history.

KINGS AND QUEENS

Henry VIII

David Fletcher

St. Martin's Press/New York
Wayland Publishers Limited/Hove, England

Copyright © 1976 by Wayland Publishers Limited
First published in the UK in 1976 by
Wayland Publishers Limited, 49 Lansdowne Place,
Hove, Sussex BN3 1HS
SBN 85340 430 5

First published in the USA in 1977
All rights reserved. For information, write:
St. Martin's Press, Inc., 175 Fifth Avenue,
New York, N.Y. 10010
Library of Congress Catalog Card Number: 77-283

Printed in Great Britain by
The Pitman Press, Bath

Library of Congress Cataloging in Publication Data
Fletcher, David, 1940-
  Henry VIII.

  Bibliography: p.
  Includes index.
  SUMMARY: The life and reign of the sixteenth-century English monarch who effected the separation of England from the Church of Rome.

  1. Henry VIII, King of England, 1491-1547—Juvenile literature. 2. Great Britain—Kings and rulers—Biography—Juvenile literature. 3. Great Britain—History—Henry VIII, 1509-1547—Juvenile literature. [1. Henry VIII, King of England, 1491-1547. 2. Kings and rulers] I. Title.
DA332.F56 1977 942.05′2′0924 [B] [92] 77-283
ISBN 0-312-36802-X

Contents

1	The Young King	7
2	The First Years on the Throne	11
3	Into Europe	16
4	The Rise of Wolsey	21
5	Peace in Europe	25
6	The Other Side of Henry	30
7	Disquiet in Henry's Mind	35
8	The King's Great Matter	40
9	The Break with Rome	45
10	Henry Feels his Strength	51
11	One Queen after Another	55
12	Newfound Riches	59
13	Henry in his Prime	64
14	Henry and his New Queen	69
15	Henry's Last Wives	74
16	War and Death	78
17	Henry, King and Emperor	85
	The Six Wives of Henry VIII	89
	Principal Characters	90
	Table of Dates	93
	Index	95
	Further Reading	96
	Picture Credits	96

1 The Young King

FOR NEARLY twenty-four years England had been ruled by Henry VII (1485–1509). Henry Tudor had won the throne from Richard III on the battlefield of Bosworth on 22nd August 1485. Bosworth was to mark the last violent change of monarchy for more than a hundred years. Yet in the century before, England had suffered some of the most violent years of her history. The rivalry between the two great dynasties of York and Lancaster in the Wars of the Roses led to a constant struggle for the throne of England which seriously weakened royal authority. Henry VII had believed it his duty to ensure, above all, that England's king should die in his bed and pass on the throne to his son without fear of civil strife.

Henry VII had achieved just this. A careful and diligent monarch, he avoided war. His reign is often seen as dull and uneventful, particularly compared to that of his son. Certainly, in the years following the death of his wife Queen Elizabeth (1465–1503), he had become increasingly cold and gloomy. He kept himself to himself and there was no hint of jollity at court in these years. Also, his own health was in serious decline. At Eastertime in 1509 he was taken seriously ill. On 22nd April he died, bequeathing to his teenage son, now Henry VIII, royal coffers lined with gold and an unchallenged title to the English throne.

On that chill April morning when people learned that the old Tudor King was dead, many questions began to trouble them. What sort of king would the young Henry prove to be? What use would he make of his father's hard work? What policy would he adopt towards England and the Continent? Would he keep the peace?

> "The wealth and civilisation of the world are here; and those who call the English barbarians appear to me to render themselves such. I here perceive very elegant manners, extreme decorum and great politeness; and amongst other things there is this invincible King, whose acquirements and qualities are so many and excellent, that I consider him to excel all who ever wore a crown." *Francisco Chieregato, the Pope's representative in England.*

Left Henry VII, represented on a silver groat (a small coin of very little value used in the sixteenth century).

Above Henry VII, father of Henry VIII.

Below Prince Arthur, eldest child of Henry VII and elder brother of Henry VIII.

One factor was very worrying to the councillors appointed to serve the new king; Prince Henry had received no instructions in the art of government. Henry was not his father's eldest son and had spent much of his early life overshadowed by the heir apparent, Prince Arthur (1486–1502). At the age of fifteen Arthur had been sent to Ludlow to gain political experience as president of a council in charge of the Welsh border. Even after Arthur's sudden death in 1502, Henry VII gave no sign of wishing to give the same kind of experience to his younger son and heir Henry.

We know rather little of Henry's upbringing. He seems to have led a very sheltered life between his birth in the royal palace at Greenwich on 28th June 1491 and his accession in 1509. Henry VII kept his son under constant care and scrutiny. The boy could only enter his own room by going through his father's chambers. If he went out he was chaperoned by trusted guards. He was forbidden to speak in public and was so cowed that he was only heard to speak in answer to his father. With the new King so little known his ability to govern must obviously be in question.

But whatever people feared about the future they soon noticed a pleasant change in the atmosphere at court. The physique and the age of the two men were so different. The old King had looked frail and worn. His son on the other hand was barely eighteen. Everyone commented on his superb physique. He looked graceful. He did daily exercises to keep fit. There was not an ounce of surplus fat. He was clean shaven and had a very delicate complexion with auburn hair. Above all he soon displayed a striking personality that made its mark on all who met him. England's new King was clearly someone to look out for.

A King so striking, youthful and handsome as Henry must surely have a wife to escort him. In fact he had a bride waiting for him but his father had not let him marry. This was Catherine of Aragon (1485–1536), daughter of King Ferdinand and Queen Isabella of Spain. Catherine had been brought over eight years before in 1501 to marry Henry's elder brother, Prince Arthur. After four months of marriage Arthur had died. Henry VII did not want to let Catherine go home, and risk losing the friendship of Spain; nor did he want to lose the promise of a big wedding dowry. He therefore proposed that she should marry her brother-in-law, Henry, who was then 14. But the Church decreed that to marry one's brother-in-law was unlawful. Catherine insisted that her marriage to Arthur had never been consummated. But this was not sufficient proof and so a special dispensation from the Pope was sought. This was granted, but when the wedding dowry from Spain failed to arrive, Henry refused to let the wedding take place However, when he died, the younger Henry felt free of all this and decided to marry Catherine just the same.

The royal marriage took place on 11th June 1509. Catherine was six years older than Henry and was now in her twenty-third year. She was small compared to her husband; she was dainty and graceful with fine eyes and a delicate complexion. Catherine had been kept waiting for the best part of ten years for one or other of her husbands. Henry too looked forward to getting married. Catherine would not only make a worthy companion for a King, but be a future mother to his children and help carry on the royal line of Tudor. The royal pair showed genuine signs of affection and love for each other; they seemed to everyone like "two love birds" adding an air of romance to all the excitement and expectation of the new reign.

Henry VIII's coronation followed some eighteen days later. It was a magnificent affair. The long procession passed through the streets of London draped with cloth of gold; Henry's costume was the most fantastic of all the lavish outfits on display. The coronation feast was "greater than any Caesar had known." Afterwards the guests went to watch a tournament that lasted until dusk. Jousts and feasts continued for many days afterwards. "Our time is spent in continuous festival," wrote Catherine to her father, Ferdinand of Spain. Noisy laughter filled the corridors of power. Gone were the

Above Catherine of Aragon, first wife of Henry VIII.

"His majesty is the handsomest potentate I ever set eyes on: above the usual height, with an extremely fine calf to his leg, his complexion very fair and bright, with auburn hair combed straight and short, in the French fashion, and a face so round and beautiful, that it would become a pretty woman, his throat being rather long and thick." *Pasqualigo, a Venetian diplomat writing in 1515.*

Above The coronation of Henry and Catherine of Aragon. A woodcut of 1509.

> "If I should declare what pain, labour and diligence the tailors, embroiderers and goldsmiths took both to make and devise garments for lords, ladies, knights and esquires and also for decking, trapping and adorning of coursers, jeunets and palfreys [all these are horses] it were too long to rehearse: but for a surety, more rich, nor more strange, nor more curious works hath not been seen than were prepared for this coronation." *Edward Hall, writing of the coronation of Henry and Catherine.*

days of sobriety, the evenings of boredom, spent under the old regime.

Yet amid all this merrymaking Henry showed that he could act with sudden and surprising savagery. His father's great fortune had largely been amassed through the diligence of two men, Richard Eupson and Edmund Dudley. No tax collector is ever popular, and these two were among the most hated men of the realm. Wishing to play the popular hero, Henry ordered them to the Tower of London and eventually had them executed. For all the warmth and glamour that he displayed there seemed to be a lack of genuine feeling for the people, a certain coldness and vanity which make for a complex, intriguing, and at times deeply disquieting personality.

2 The First Years on the Throne

Left Henry sitting in Parliament with his Council.

IN HIS FIRST YEARS as King, Henry was content to leave affairs of state in the hands of the wise noblemen who had served his father. A Council, rather like our modern Cabinet, advised the King. It consisted of middle-aged men committed to the first Tudor's policy of peace abroad and law and order at home. Dominant among them was William Warham (1450–1532), Archbishop of Canterbury, and Thomas Ruthell, Bishop of Durham. The leading member of the Council was Richard Fox (1448?–1528), Bishop of Winchester. Such was Fox's influence that in these first years of Henry's reign he was often referred to as the "other king". Thanks to the influence of these men there was no drastic break from the policy set by Henry's father. England for the moment

remained at peace.

The old men of the Council seemed very capable, and the young King was content to leave the business of government to them and indulge his newfound power. The years following Henry's accession saw a continuation of the revels surrounding his wedding and coronation. Formal entertainments were held throughout the year on red-letter days such as royal birthdays and religious festivals. On these occasions the court transformed itself into a make-believe world and usually acted out some romantic story of knights-in-armour and maidens in distress. On New Year's Eve in 1512 Henry decided to play at wooing ladies from a tower. To achieve the best effect a mock castle fully equipped with gates, towers and artillery, was brought into the hall. Henry and five of his courtiers—magnificently dressed in parti-coloured coats, half of russet satin, half of cloth of gold—came in and began to assault the castle. The ladies at first would not yield, but after some gentle persuasion they came out with the King and company. After the dance it was the ladies' turn to do the enticing. They returned to the castle with the knights following. The gates were shut and the castle was removed from court.

Some six days later on Twelfth Night Henry and eleven courtiers came into court disguised in "garments long and broad wrought all with gold and vizors and caps of gold." Later "they desired the ladies to dance . . . and after they danced and communed together they took their leave."

The popular idea of "Bluff King Hal" is fostered by events such as these and by his sudden appearances in public or among friends, in disguise. Though jousting played a part in the coronation celebrations, Henry did not indulge in the sport; but early next year he was tempted to try his hand. He appeared incognito in a private joust at Richmond early in 1510. After defeating his opponent he lifted his vizor to reveal his true identity—much to the surprise of the audience. Again a few days later he "invaded" Queen Catherine's chambers with a dozen friends dressed in Kentish green and

Above Archbishop Warham, one of the leaders of Henry's Council.

"The King and eleven courtiers were disguised after the manner of Italy, called a mask, a thing not seen before in England. They were apparelled in garments long and broad, wrought all with gold, with vizers and caps of gold; and after the banquet done, the maskers came in with six gentlemen disguised in silk, bearing staff torches, and desired the ladies to dance. And after they danced and communed together, they took their leave and departed." *A contemporary description of the Twelfth Night Celebration in 1512.*

Top left A court dance, from a contemporary engraving. *Bottom left* Henry taking part in one of his court spectaculars.

Above Henry hunting in Epping Forest.

"The guests remained at table for seven hours by the clock. All the viands placed before the King were borne by an 'elephant' or by 'lions' or 'panthers' or other 'animals' marvellously designed. Every imaginable sort of meat known in the Kingdom was served, and fish in like manner, even down to prawn pasties. But the jellies of some twenty sorts perhaps, surpassed everything, being made in the shape of castles and animals of various descriptions, as beautiful and as admirable as can be imagined." *An Italian visitor's description of one of Henry's banquets early in his reign.*

carrying bows and arrows pretending to be Robin Hood and his merry men. Catherine and her ladies were very alarmed and not until they had danced around the room did the King, to their relief, take off his disguise.

Henry was always anxious to appear a popular and likeable figure. In complete contrast to his stern father he took every opportunity to show himself to his subjects. Instead of keeping the court at London where few could see it he began to tour the country, especially in the summer months. He like the countryside, and hunting and hawking were among his favourite pleasures. During the royal hunt the public would be invited to watch and were given a taste of the king's food afterwards at the royal banquet.

These first years on the throne were great fun for Henry. Money flowed endlessly from the royal coffers. He wanted to enjoy himself. After all those years of strict control by his father he was intoxicated with freedom, and the exhilaration of being King. The power, so carefully nurtured by his father, went a little to his head.

Henry had a striking manner, especially in his dress. His fingers were a mass of jewelled rings. Around his neck he wore a golden collar from which "hung a diamond as big as a walnut". His clothes were in keeping with this finery, woven of sumptuous silks and cloths of gold. He thought nothing of paying out £335 to a Paris jeweller or £560 for a thousand pearls. In 1511, New Year presents alone set him back some £800. It is hard to translate such figures into modern terms, but to multiply them by thirty will give a rough idea of Henry's extravagance.

Yet for all this high-living we should never doubt the sincerity and earnestness with which Henry viewed his office as King. One problem always uppermost in his mind—as it had been in his father's—was that of leaving his son an unchallenged inheritance. First, of course, he needed an heir and it seemed as if this little problem would soon be over because on New Year's Day, 1511, Queen Catherine gave birth to a son.

Henry was delighted. The magnificent pageants and tournaments that were put on rivalled even those of his coronation. He wore gorgeous costumes with "H" and "K" in gold thread embroidered on his back. Such was his high-spirited excitement that he let the crowds rip the letters off his back as royal keepsakes. Providence was surely smiling on his new reign. In thankfulness he rode out to the shrine of Our Lady at Walsingham in Norfolk on a pilgrimage of thanksgiving.

Yet such was the slender thread of infant life in the sixteenth century that within two months the little hope of England, and of Henry, was dead. Henry was heartbroken.

But he and his Queen were still young and he consoled himself with the thought that other offspring would follow. Besides, his mind was now beginning to turn toward thoughts of war. The delights of the joust and tournament were fine enough, but they had a more serious purpose as the training ground of future soldiers. With dreams of reliving the glory of Henry V (1387–1422) and his conquests in France, Henry resolved to cast aside his father's cautious foreign policy and plunge into the internal politics of Europe.

> "He [Henry] is very fond of hunting, and never takes his diversion without tiring eight or ten horses which he causes to be stationed beforehand along the line of country he means to take, and when one is tired he mounts another, and before he gets home they are all exhausted. He is extremely fond of tennis, at which game it is the prettiest thing in the world to see him play, his fair skin glowing through a shirt of the finest texture." *Pasqualigo, a Venetian diplomat, writing in 1515.*

3 Into Europe

Below Louis XII, who was King of France when Henry came to the throne of England.

IN THE EARLY 1500s Europe was dominated by three main power groups. In the south there was the Pope, head of the Church but also a powerful prince ruling a large part of Italy. Controlling most of central Europe was the Emperor Maximilian (1459–1519), while to the far west his brother Ferdinand (1452–1516) was King in Spain. Between the lands of these two brothers lay France with Louis XII (1462–1515) as its king. The story of European politics at this time is one of a constant struggle between these rival groups for supremacy. First it would be the turn of Louis XII (the house of Valois) and then the Emperor (the house of Hapsburg) to assert his strength only to be countered by an attack by his rival. These monarchs of late mediaeval Europe were old, crafty and full of the ways of the world. Henry of England was very young and inexperienced by comparison. But he wanted to join this exclusive circle.

Henry had wanted to plunge England into a European conflict right at the start of his reign. He wished to follow the traditional policy of English kings of being anti-French and to wage a war to reclaim the crown of France for himself. He showed his contempt for the gout-ridden Louis XII by insulting the French ambassador who came to pay his respects. But Henry had to wait three years before he could get a campaign against France under way.

The Council, or inner cabinet, of advisers remembered the peaceful policy of Henry VII and felt it should continue. They even sent a letter to Louis, without telling Henry, proposing a further period of peace. Having no idea of the original letter when he received Louis' reply, Henry was furious, but for the moment he reluctantly accepted their advice and bided his time.

He would not have long to wait. Sooner or later the old Hapsburg-Valois rivalry would flare up again in Europe. Also inside the Council itself was a small but influential group, led by the Duke of Norfolk (1443–1524), which favoured war. Two years after his accession the rumours of war, even in faraway Italy, were enough to give Henry an excuse to enter the European scene.

Italy at this time was a collection of independent states, not the united country we know today. Some of these states were rich and important, and coveted by the major powers of northern Europe. In particular Venice was looked on as a prize for France. Pope Julius II (1443–1513) became alarmed at this prospect because it would mean that his own territory would inevitably become weaker and fall under French influence.

The Pope's cries of alarm did not fall on deaf ears. Ferdinand of Spain had for years wanted to capture the French town of Navarre. He thought that his chance to do this, by joining in an attack on France, had now come. Henry was very pro-Pope. He had been raised in the Catholic faith and saw the Pope as the supreme spiritual authority. When the crafty Ferdinand convinced Henry that France was about to attack Italy, he was only too keen to enter the Holy League of Spain, Venice and the Pope. Henry signed the treaty on 13th November 1511, and four days later committed himself to attack France before the end of 1512.

Here was the chance to win back England's lost empire on the continent. Less than a century before, roughly half of France paid tribute to the English king. All that was left of this once vast empire was one coastal town, Calais. However, with this fresh opportunity and all France to play for, why should the lost empire not be regained?

In May 1512 with a mixture of pride, anxiety and excitement Henry bade his troops *bon-voyage* as they prepared to join the Spanish forces in southern France. Some 12,000 troops sailed under the command of the Marquess of Dorset. They arrived at the port of

Top Ferdinand I of Spain; *below* his brother, the Emperor Maximilian I. Maximilian had control of most of central Europe when Henry became King, while Ferdinand and Louis XII controlled the two other major European powers, Spain and France.

Below The *pavis*, a popular siege weapon in the time of Henry VIII. The *pavis* was simply a large shield protecting the whole body.

Fuenterrabia on 7th June 1512. Here they waited for the Spanish army to show itself, to have a joint force to penetrate French territory and attack Bayonne. They waited and waited but the Spanish army never arrived. Unknown to the Marquess of Dorset the Spaniards had already attacked and captured the territory of Navarre. Ferdinand had got what he wanted and declared a truce. Ignorant of these events Dorset waited for four months until at last, frustrated, tired and near to mutiny, his army made its weary and forlorn way home.

Henry was humiliated; but he was determined to reverse the fortunes of the first campaign. The Pope gave Henry every incentive to chance his luck once more in Europe. The Pope was eager to pursue the struggle against France, and Henry—the dutiful son of the Church—was only too keen to help him. Perhaps the dismal fortunes of the first campaign could be reversed. This time Henry would have as an ally not only Ferdinand of Spain, but also Emperor Maximilian. In March 1513 Maximilian had been persuaded to join the Holy League. However, Ferdinand's support was once again non-existent. He made a secret deal with France which left him in control of Navarre and then backed out of the struggle. The young King of England was learning fast in this ruthless game of international politics. He had been let down badly by Ferdinand of Spain; distrustful of his motives Henry decided to lead the next expedition himself. He would use as a bridgehead for his attack on France the town of Calais, and make himself as independent as possible from Spanish support.

It was a glittering spectacle as the English army set foot on French soil on 30th June 1513. Henry did not forego any of his luxuries even when leading an army into war. Some three hundred people catered for his personal needs—servants, cooks, groomsmen, secretaries, advisers and ministers. Henry even brought over his own choirboys to sing in the services conducted by his priests. There was only one element of court life missing—the ladies. Indeed, if they had been present the English court might well have been on one of its summer expeditions into the countryside.

After three weeks of festivities, jousting and tournaments, they at last felt ready for the real thing and marched off into French territory. On this first section of the march the rain poured down. Henry refused to be daunted; he rode around in drenched clothes cheering up his troops as they pitched camp in the mud. Henry was determined to keep morale as high as possible. By 1st August 1513 his army was encamped around the walls of Theouranne. Here they set about besieging the town. The French held out until, on 16th August, there happened a victory which Henry had long been praying for. A group of French cavalry had misjudged its position and in a moment of panic had turned and fled. This "Battle of the Spurs" was aptly named, for spurs were the only weapons used by the French as they urged on their horses to outrun the pursuing English army. Elated by their success the English pressed home their advantage. On 24th August Theouranne fell. To punish its obstinacy in refusing to surrender Henry ordered the town to be razed to the ground.

The English army next turned its attention to the French town of Tournai which capitulated on 21st September 1513, though Henry decided that this fine old town should be spared. At a stroke, England's continental possessions had been doubled. After three weeks of jousting and merrymaking Henry returned home in triumph on 21st October 1513.

While Henry had been on the continent trouble had been brewing at home. James IV (1473–1513) of Scotland had renewed the "auld alliance" between Scotland and France. He was married to Henry's sister Margaret, but he preferred to rally to the cause of Louis XII than to his brother-in-law. After several hints as to what might happen, James IV marched south over the River Tweed to do battle with the English. On the 9th September 1513 the two armies of Scotland and England met at Flodden in a bloody and terrible encounter. In three hours it was all over. The English were undisputed masters of the field. Most of the Scottish

"The English did not trouble themselves with prisoners, but slew and stripped King, bishops, lords and nobles and left them naked on the field." *Eyewitness account of the Battle of Flodden.*

Below A battering-ram in use in a siege.

Above left James IV, King of Scotland, defeated at the Battle of Flodden, *(top right)* by the English army in 1513.

"Then out burst the ordnance on both sides with fire flame and hideous noises: and the master-gunner of the English slew the master-gunner of Scotland and beat all his men from his guns, so that the Scottish ordnance did no harm to the Englishmen, but the Englishmen's artillery shot into the King's battard, slew many persons."
Eyewitness account of the Battle of Flodden.

aristocracy, including twelve earls, an archbishop and two bishops lay dead. Most important of all the Scottish King himself lay slain on the battlefield. This was a shattering defeat for Scotland. For Henry it was of far greater value than any of his victories in France. All Henry had from his French expedition was one town, Tournai. An embarrassing luxury, it proved far too expensive to keep up, and in 1518 it was gladly given back to the French. Yet here was Scotland, without any great expense, completely at Henry's feet. Here was the possibility of an invasion and an eventual integration of Scotland into the kingdom. But Henry missed his chance. His eyes were still glued on the Continent. The Emperor Maximilian dropped strong hints to Henry that he would not prevent him becoming King of France. With this in mind the cold, bleak Scottish landscape seemed a second best.

The battles of 1513 were to prove the last for a decade. Within two years Henry's younger sister Mary, by general consent the most attractive lady at court, was married to the old and crippled King Louis of France. This sudden change in policy towards France and the substitution of peace for war in Europe was the handiwork of one remarkable man—Thomas Wolsey.

4 The Rise of Wolsey

THOMAS WOLSEY (1475–1530) dominated the first half of Henry's reign. He stands, in every respect, as big and as important as the King himself. In many of their characteristics they were alike. Wolsey was a big and corpulent man as Henry himself became in old age. Both men liked food and ate to excess. Both were extroverts with a love of colourful display and the levers of power. Wolsey was ambitious and rose to power quickly, but no matter how high he climbed he was always regarded as an upstart by the aristocratic members of the court.

Thomas Wolsey was the son of an Ipswich butcher. To anyone of ambition and of humble birth the Church offered one of the few roads to advancement. Life was much shorter in the sixteenth century than it is today. A man was considered old at fifty. People were married and received their education much earlier than we do. Wolsey took his B.A. degree at Oxford University at the age of fifteen. Such was his promise that he was elected a fellow of his college, but his eyes were on prizes political rather than academic. In 1507 he was appointed chaplain to Henry VII. When Henry VIII came to the throne he appointed him his adviser. The new King was very impressed by Wolsey's diligence and hard work. In 1513 Wolsey was given the task of organizing the campaign in France.

This was Wolsey's breakthrough. Such was the success of the French campaign that Henry could not heap enough honours and titles on him. In August 1514 Wolsey was appointed Archbishop of York. Soon afterwards the bishopric of Tournai was offered to him. Following pressure from Henry, the Pope in 1515 created Wolsey a Cardinal. Henry further rewarded

"Acquiring so many offices at almost the same time, he became so proud that he began to regard himself as the equal of Kings. Soon he began to use a golden seat, a golden cushion, a golden cloth on his table. Thus Wolsey, with his arrogance and ambition aroused against himself the hatred of the whole country, and by his hostility towards the nobility and the common people, caused them the greatest irritation through his vainglory." *Polydore Vergil, History of England.*

Above Cardinal Wolsey with his train. Wolsey was a man of great wealth and power in his prime, and his stature rivalled even that of the King.

Wolsey by appointing him Lord Chancellor, an office not unlike that of a modern Prime Minister. A few years later the Pope made him his Legate (personal representative) in England. Other bishoprics followed and in 1521 he became Abbot of St. Albans, the richest monastery in England. Never before had one person amassed so much wealth.

Within a few months of becoming Archbishop of York Wolsey took a ninety-nine year lease on the manor at Hampton Court and began building a great house for himself. He had chosen a site well away from the smoke and plagues of London. Using his influence and wealth he engaged the best craftsmen in Europe to create a residence worthy of a Cardinal. Both in its up-to-date amenities, with its sewage and fresh water conveyed through lead pipes, and its rich furnishings, his palace was acknowledged to be the finest in the realm.

Wolsey's whole style of life became regal. He began to

"Who was now in high favour, but Master Almoner? And who ruled all under the King, but Master Almoner?"
Life and Death of Cardinal Wolsey, George Cavendish.

Left Cardinal Wolsey, by an unknown artist.

Above The opening of Parliament in 1515. Wolsey is seated two to the right of the King, with the Cardinal's hat above his head.

"Why come ye not to court?
To which court?
To the King's court,
Or to Hampton Court?
Nay, to the King's Court!
The King's court
should have the excellence
But Hampton Court
Hath the preeminence
And York's Place
With my Lord's Grace!
To whom magnificence
Is all the confluence,
Suits and supplication,
Embassades of all nations."

Part of a poem by John Skelton (1460?–1529) who was very critical of the Church and of Wolsey in particular.

outshine Henry himself. In processions two great crosses of silver were carried before him to symbolize his two great offices of Archbishop of York and of Legate. The symbol of his other great office of Lord Chancellor, the great seal, was carried in a silk purse by a page walking behind his master. Wolsey liked to ride on a white mule symbolizing humility. Ironically, the mule was decked out with costly gold and red trappings. Wolsey had nearly a thousand personal servants. Each servant wore the Cardinal's distinctive livery of crimson velvet embroidered with the insignia of a cardinal's hat. Wolsey even outdid the King in his gifts to the poor. The food given to the poor at the gates of Hampton Court made the relief offered at royal palaces seem mean by comparison.

This magnificence, however, was well earned in Henry's opinion, and he felt no jealousy for his able Cardinal. Wolsey was a man of industry and thrived on hard work, a quality much admired by Henry. Wolsey was a born administrator and he had a voracious appetite for ministerial paperwork. He could work for amazingly long hours. The Venetian ambassador in London said he could carry out, single-handed, all the business which filled the offices and courts of Venice. Henry VIII was frankly bored by business routine and quite willing to let Wolsey handle it, leaving himself time to pursue life's more enjoyable aspects. Wolsey himself revelled in this increased power. One courtier noted his change of style of address over the years. Wolsey had begun by saying, "His majesty will do so and so," then it became, "We shall do so and so," and finally "I shall do so and so."

Yet for all Wolsey's arrogance and claims to quasi-regal status Henry was still master. As long as Wolsey obeyed Henry was satisfied. There might come a time when Wolsey would fail him, but for the moment Henry was content to leave affairs of state to his able Cardinal.

5 Peace in Europe

WOLSEY'S foreign policy was designed to give England the balance of power in Europe. After Henry's successes at Tournai and Flodden England was respected in the courts of Europe. Wolsey built on this strength to establish peaceful relations with France while still keeping on friendly terms with the Emperor Maximilian. It was not easy. The difficulty lay in England's relationship with France. Mutual ties with the Empire, particularly by the export of wool through the Empire's Netherlands ports, made many Englishmen look upon the Empire as their natural ally. The traditional enemy for years had been France.

However an Anglo-French understanding was made easier by Henry's recent victories. Louis XII acknowledged Henry's triumph and agreed to pay him a large annual pension and accept the loss of Tournai. The alliance was sealed with the marriage of Henry's younger sister, Mary Tudor, to Louis. It was a cruel and entirely political marriage between a beautiful girl and a gouty, toothless and depraved old man; but it was softened somewhat by Henry's promise to Mary that she could marry the man of her choice when Louis died. She did not have long to wait. The excitement and festivities of his marriage to a young girl proved too much for him, and within eleven weeks he was dead. The Anglo-French alliance was again in jeopardy. It was to be Wolsey's task to win the friendship of the new King, Francis I (1494–1597).

Francis was a slightly younger man than Henry and at once a jealous rivalry seemed to mark them both. Henry

Below Francis I, who became King of France when Louis XII died. As a young and handsome king he aroused Henry's jealousy.

> "The King is extremely handsome. Nature could not have done more for him. He is much handsomer than any sovereign in Christendom—a great deal handsomer than the King of France, very fair and his whole frame admirably proportioned." *Compliment paid to Henry by one of his courtiers.*

was very curious to know what Francis looked like. He was sure that no one could have such a fine physique as he had. Or could they? Once he inquired about the size of Francis's leg, but without waiting for a reply he opened the front of his doublet and slapped his thigh: no monarch could boast of such legs as Henry! Henry's suspicions of Francis' physique were justified. He is described by the Bishop of Worcester as "tall in stature, broad shouldered, oval and handsome in face, very slender in the legs and much inclined to corpulence"—a mirror image of Henry.

But both monarchs, and certainly Wolsey, wanted to hold on to the peace of the past few years. Peace was the cornerstone of Wolsey's policy; the highlight of his career came when representatives of the Pope, the Emperor, the King of Spain, King of France and King of England all met in London and agreed to make a united effort to turn the Turk out of Palestine and to include in their treaty all the other powers of Europe, Denmark, Scotland, Hungary, the Italian States and Switzerland. Here was a treaty of universal peace; for Wolsey it was a diplomatic triumph of the first order.

London had been the city chosen for this meeting and Wolsey the man to officiate. On 3rd October 1518 a High Mass was held in St. Paul's Cathedral in thanksgiving for peace. The service was a splendid affair matched only by Wolsey's hospitality afterwards. There is no record of the meal given by Henry after the service but the state banquet given by Wolsey later that night was more sumptuous than any feast "given by Cleopatra or Caligula." London was now the hub of European diplomacy and Wolsey had realized his dream to be "the arbiter of Christendom."

One important outcome of this gathering was the decision of the French and English ambassadors that Henry and Francis should meet. As a token of his regard for Francis, Henry swore not to shave until they met. Unfortunately Henry had not reckoned with his wife. Catherine hated beards, so Henry dutifully shaved it off. Henry's affection for Catherine still came before Anglo-

> "Nothing pleases him [Wolsey] more than to be called the arbiter of the affairs of Christendom." *The Venetian Ambassador writing shortly after the London Conference.*

French relations.

Before the two monarchs met in the spring of 1519 an interesting court purge took place. Henry always had around him a small group of men of his own age. He liked good-humoured company, and over the years this group of friends had formed themselves into an exclusive club. They jousted, played tennis and gambled together. The older members of the court did not take kindly to them and thought that their behaviour was beneath the dignity of a king. These young courtiers had recently visited the court of Francis I. The French court was far more lax and boisterous than Henry's and these courtiers, among other things, had gone with Francis through the streets of Paris throwing eggs and vegetables at the people in the streets. They came home and began to do the same things in London.

This was taking things too far. The Council met and asked Henry to put a stop to their wild behaviour. The King agreed. The young courtiers were sent away and their places taken by "four sound and ancient knights." The time had come to stop playing games, and show more interest in the affairs of state. Wolsey was still in charge but Henry became much more active now in politics.

The day was near for Henry and Francis to meet. Because of his organizing ability Wolsey was to arrange the meeting. The site chosen in France was the Val d'Or, the Field of Cloth of Gold. This has given its name to the meeting. It is an apt title. The Field of Cloth of Gold was far more than just another political conference. It was to consist of an athletics' meeting; a festival of music and a series of banquets; a splendid occasion for both courts to show off their wealth and prestige. Both sides wished to outdo the other in costumes, equipment, food and drink. It was to be the eighth wonder of the world.

The entire English court sailed across the Channel to attend on the King. Henry VIII's retinue alone numbered some 3,997 persons and together with Queen Catherine's servants more than 5,000 people attended the royal pleasure. These servants were all decked out in

Below The Man-of-War in which Henry sailed from Dover in 1520 for his meeting with Francis I at Val d'Or.

Above The meeting of Henry VIII and Francis I at Val d'Or. In this detail from a narrative painting, showing several events happening at once, Henry can be seen arriving with his retinue.

the most sumptuous velvets, satin and cloth of gold. Besides this large human contingent, nearly 3,000 horses were shipped over to France.

Wolsey felt that the splendour of all this reflected on himself, and he worried over every detail. Some 6,000 workmen prepared the city of coloured tents that would house the visiting courtiers. Tons of provisions were wanted, too. Everything the court could possibly need was shipped over—7,000 conger eels, 2,014 sheep, 26 dozen heron, 4 bushels of mustard and £1.0.10d. worth of cream for the King's cakes; chestfuls of crockery, cutlery and glass.

In the first week of June 1520 the final details were completed. The day for the auspicious meeting, 7th June, had arrived. It was a tense moment. As the two Kings rode towards each other, each flanked by their supporters, it was as if two armies were riding against each other. After years of national rivalry, and the jealousy of the two monarchs, both sides feared treachery, perhaps a bloody ambush. The horn sounded and the two Kings left their followers, met and embraced. It was a moment of great relief. The words of friendship had been genuine after all, and the monarchs' embrace was the signal for two weeks of furious merrymaking.

Wine flowed freely in the streets and food was in superabundance. There were jousts and tournaments, and the strict code of chivalry was adhered to. Henry and Francis avoided open competition, but Francis did once propose that they should wrestle. Henry took up the challenge and was promptly flung on his back. This was quickly forgotten by all the English observers, but not surprisingly every French chronicler records the incident.

The end of the meeting was marked by a Mass sung on 23rd June 1520. Both English and French choirs sang, to symbolize the new understanding between the two countries. It was also suggested that a chapel should be built and dedicated to Our Lady of Friendships and jointly maintained by the Kings of England and of France, but it was never built. The meeting had been arranged against a background of uncertainty in European politics. In 1517 the ageing Emperor Maximilian had suffered a stroke. It would not be long before he died. His obvious successor was his grandson Charles, but the title was an elected and not a hereditary one. Francis thought he had at least a chance, however slight, of gaining enough votes to make him the next Emperor. So from the time of Maximilian's illness to the eventual election of Charles in 1519 as the next Emperor everyone had been looking around for support.

By the time of the Field of Cloth of Gold the election was already over; Francis was already thinking of war and a way to avenge himself against his rival Charles V (1519–55). Henry VIII was having secret talks with Charles, urged on by Wolsey who clearly saw that the one great prize that eluded him—the Papacy itself—could be gained with Charles's help rather than Francis's. Within two years of the Field of Cloth of Gold Europe was again at war and Henry supported Charles in his struggle against the King of France.

All the extravagance of this meeting came to nothing. It was as shallow and costly as it was inappropriate and ineffective.

6 The Other Side of Henry

HENRY VIII had a good appetite for fun; he enjoyed a good joke and outdoor life in addition to his love of making war, and trying to impose his will on all around him. In a word he was an extrovert. But there is another side to Henry's character—that of the scholar and the musician—which makes him one of the most learned and talented of all the kings of England.

Henry's father was no intellectual, but he was a great patron of the arts and learning who liked to have clever people about him. Henry's grandmother, Lady Margaret Beaufort (1443–1509) was probably responsible for his education. She was the most influential person at court in fostering the arts, and was herself a great patron of learning. Her greatest memorials are two colleges at Cambridge (Christ's College and St. John's) which she helped to create. She saw to it that Henry had the best possible tutors from his father's court. As a young boy he learned Latin, French and some Italian. Later on he acquired some Spanish and in 1519 even began to learn Greek. He was also good enough at mathematics to be able to converse with the authorities of the day.

Henry was perhaps most talented in music. He was fond of all kinds, from plainsong and church anthems to love songs and bawdy drinking songs. He had a good singing voice and could play the lute, organ and other keyboard instruments. He was a prolific composer and his compositions show his varied interest—music for Church services as well as lighter music. Two of his motets, *O Lord the Maker of all things* and *Quam pulchres est*, are still performed today. He could have made a success of music if he had not been King.

Below Margaret Beaufort, Countess of Richmond and Derby, grandmother of Henry.

When Henry came to the throne he had just two minstrels. He was determined to improve the standard of music at court. He founded the "King's Music" and music of high standard became an integral part of court life. He scoured the whole of the continent, as well as England, to recruit the finest talent into his choir at the Chapel Royal. He liked music and was prepared to pay a high price for it. The incentive of a high salary encouraged many musicians to come to court. They lived like gentlemen and their salary was up to three times that of a parish priest. In later years visitors from abroad wrote home praising the music they heard at Henry's court.

But Henry's most serious occupation was theology, and the scholarly study of ideas. The term "Renaissance" is used to describe the love of learning and scholarship which gripped western Europe in the early part of the sixteenth century. "Renaissance" literally means re-birth. For centuries scholars had been content to unravel and argue over small points of dogma and theology; but now there was a renewal of interest in the ancient but forgotten literatures of Greece and Rome. Philosophers, writers and painters began to throw out the old ideas and show far more interest in earthly than heavenly activities. One can see this in the paintings of the time: human figures look and are painted to be flesh and blood rather than ethereal saintly subjects symbolizing some holy ideal.

Philosophers, too, became more interested in the ways of men—hence the name "humanist" by which they were known. Chief among these was a Dutch scholar Erasmus (1466–1562) and Sir Thomas More (1478–1535). Although these men were breaking new ground the language they wrote in was still Latin. With this common language they could move easily around the courts of Europe and be understood. Erasmus spent many years in London. Such was the make-up of Henry's court that Erasmus felt quite at home there. He enjoyed talking and arguing with the King and his friends. He described Henry's court as the best universi-

"He [Henry] speaks French, English, and Latin and a little Italian, plays well on the lute and harpsichord, sings from book at sight, draws the bow with greater strength than any man in England, and jousts marvellously. Believe me, he is in every respect a most accomplished Prince." *This description was written in a despatch in 1515 by a Venetian diplomat, Pasqualigo*

"If you could see how everyone here rejoices in having so great a prince, how his life is all their desire, you would not contain yourself for sheer joy. Extortion is put down, liberality scatters riches with a bountiful hand, yet our King does not set his heart on gold or jewels, but on virtue, glory and immortality. The other day he told me, 'I wish I were more learned.' 'But learning is not what we expect of a King,' I answered, 'merely that he should encourage scholars.' 'Most certainly,' he said 'as without them we should scarcely live at all.' Now what more splendid remark could a prince make?" Lord Mountjoy writing in 1509 to his friend Erasmus in Italy of the intellectual climate in Henry's court.

ty in Europe and wrote that there were in London "five or six excellent scholars who have not their equal in Italy."

Thomas More was fast becoming one of the most noteworthy scholars in Europe; he was equally at home in Henry's court. As he wrote later, Henry VIII would take him "into his private room and there some time in matter of astronomy, geometry, divinity and such other faculties, and some time in his worldly affairs, to sit and confer with him, and other whiles would he in the night have up unto the leads roof there to consider with him the diversities, courses, motions and operations of the stars and planets." It was not all jousting and merrymaking at Henry's court.

The Church had for centuries dominated the lives of men. For some time vague rumblings had been heard that the Church was too lax and ought to put its house in order. Aided by the renewed interest in learning, men began to take a more critical view of the Church and a cry for reform gained momentum. It came to a climax when in 1517 a young German monk Martin Luther (1483–1546) boldly fixed to the door of Wittenberg Cathedral a list of grievances against the Catholic Church.

Luther declared that the Church had become slovenly and too worldly in its ways. The priest had become too powerful, and the services too complicated and ponderous for ordinary folk to follow. It was time for the priest to give up much of his authority and, as a sign, his elaborate vestments. To denote his manhood, and to be like other men, he should be allowed to marry. The church building, too, itself should be divested of most of its ornaments, candles and embroidered tapestries to be more in line with the simple teaching of Christ. Instead of the Mass and other services, Luther thought that the Bible should be the pivot of all Church teaching, and its method the sermon. To make sure that everything was understood the Bible and all Church services should be in the people's native tongue rather than Latin, which was the official language of the Church. Many people agreed with him.

Germany at this time was a collection of small independent states loosely knit into the Holy Roman Empire. The teaching of Protestantism or Lutheranism appealed to many Germans. Although the Emperor Charles V refused to become a Lutheran, many German princes and their states were converted to Lutheranism. Since many of them were key trading states with the rest of Europe Lutheranism quickly spread. England's principal trading links were with the wool ports of the Netherlands, such as Amsterdam. Through them Luther's teachings began to circulate in England.

Henry VIII was a devout Catholic, and very probably died one. He may have directed the course of events that were to break the ties that linked England to the Pope but he was always a reluctant reformer. In his earlier years he was decidedly very pro-Pope. Alarmed by what he had heard of Martin Luther's teachings and the

Opposite page: left Sir Thomas More, from a copy of the portrait by Hans Holbein. *Right* Desiderius Erasmus.

"Pastime with good company
I love and shall until I die
Grudge who lust, but none deny,
So God be pleased this life will I
   For my pastance
   Hunt sing and dance
   My heart is set,
   All goodly sport
   To my comfort
   Who shall me let?"

"Youth will needs have dalliance,
Of good or ill some pastance;
Company me thinketh best
All thought and fancies to digest,
   For idleness
   Is chief mistress
   Of vices all;
   Then who can say
   But pass the day
   Is best of all?"

"Company with honesty
Is virtue—and vice to flee,
Company is good or ill
But every man hath his free will.
   The best I sue
   The worst eschew:
   My mind shall be
   Virtue to use
   Vice to refuse
   I shall use me."

"Pastime with good company" a song written by Henry.

Above Martin Luther preaching, from an illustrated manuscript of the time. In 1517 Luther set off a revolution against the Catholic Church. He then proposed his own ideas, which became the basis of the movement known as Lutheranism.

prospect of them gaining a foothold in England he prepared a counter-attack, the *Defence of the Seven Sacraments*. Most of this book is thought to be Henry's own work. With a royal author it is not surprising that it became a best-seller not only in England but all over Europe, running through some twenty editions. Here was the success Henry had so much desired in the world of scholarship. He had already proved his prowess in the tournament and in the hunt; now he could boast of a book.

He dedicated the book to the Pope. Henry had long been jealous of the title "The Most Christian King" enjoyed by the King of France and the King of Spain's too, "His Catholic Majesty." Fortunately for Henry the Pope liked the book and on 11th October 1521, bestowed on him the title "Defender of the Faith". This title was intended to be for Henry alone but it has been handed down ever since and our present Queen still bears it.

But however deep his love of learning, Henry's greatest love was of himself. To please his ego and get his own way friends like Thomas More would be ruthlessly sacrificed, his love of learning forgotten. We can attribute, if not excuse, a good deal of this decline in character to the relentless pressures and affairs of state. The second half of Henry's reign is dominated by the vexed question of his divorce from Queen Catherine. As frustrations and tensions mounted over the divorce and all that it entailed, so Henry grew more and more short tempered, and more determined to get his own way. It is to this question of the divorce and the problems of the succession that we will now turn.

7 Disquiet in Henry's Mind

BY THE MID-1520s Henry VIII had ceased to be a loving husband. Queen Catherine was still faithful and dutiful toward him. But she was five years older than Henry and she was now forty. Once good-looking and attractive, she was now a wrinkled and dumpy middle-aged woman. In the earlier years Henry had shown a great passion for her. He had jousted for her and sported her initials on his sleeve. In that glorious year of 1513 when France had seemed to be at his feet, Henry had raced back to London to offer her the keys of the French towns he had captured.

The King's sex life has been the cause of much speculation and gossip. Henry was not a Don Juan or Casanova. He was no great lover. Certainly he had mistresses and six wives, but sex was no great pleasure except in his early days. It was a duty, a duty to produce a male heir to continue the Tudor line safely into a third generation.

Catherine had failed in this. For all her pregnancies she only gave birth to one child who survived childhood, Mary (Queen of England 1553–8). When Mary was born in February 1516, the King exclaimed to the Venetian ambassador, "We are both young; if it was a daughter this time, by the grace of God the sons will follow." But no sons were born. After sixteen years of repeated pregnancies Catherine's exhausted body refused to conceive any more. It was clear to everyone that the King could not expect a male heir.

Should Henry have shared the responsibility? He thought not. After all, he had proved himself able to

Below Mary Tudor, daughter of Henry VIII and Catherine of Aragon. She became Mary I, and ruled England from 1553 to 1558.

> "If a man takes his brother's wife, it is impurity. He has brought shame upon his brother; they shall be proscribed." *Leviticus, Chapter 20, verse 21 (N.E.B.).*
>
> "You shall not have intercouse with your brother's wife; that is to bring shame upon." *Leviticus, Chapter 18, verse 16 (N.E.B.).*

father a son; in 1519 his mistress Elizabeth Blount had given birth to a boy whom Henry later made the Duke of Richmond (1519–36). But the King needed a legitimate male heir. Since those days we have Queen Elizabeth I, Queen Anne and later Victoria. But to Henry VIII the only example of a Queen of England was Matilda (1133–54) who had been a disaster and left England in a state of anarchy. Henry genuinely feared dynastic failure, and the prospect of his reign ending in civil war. A healthy male would not only solve the succession problem; it would create an atmosphere of confidence and calm at home and respect abroad. But how was this heir to be got?

Henry was a devout person and a keen student of the scriptures. That God should deny him a son, that Catherine should have had so many miscarriages and still births, surely meant that God was displeased with him. One day reading through the Book of Leviticus Henry came across the passage which condemns the man who marries his brother's wife. Yet this was exactly what Henry had done! Catherine had been married to his elder brother Prince Arthur. Could this be why God was so displeased? Some time before Catherine's fortieth birthday a "great scruple" began to haunt Henry's mind. Was he, or was he not, properly married?

The question of a divorce was first broached by Henry in 1527. One cannot question Henry's sincerity. He undoubtedly came to believe that he had been living in sin all these years, and that in the sight of God had never been married to Catherine. The Church had let him marry his brother's widow in the first place. Now the Church must undo its handiwork and get him a divorce. Henry turned to Cardinal Wolsey to sort out his problems.

When we left Wolsey he was at the height of his career following the treaty of London and the meeting of Henry and Francis at the Field of Cloth of Gold. But by 1527 Wolsey was in desperate straits. His policy of friendship with both the King of France and the Emperor had backfired. Whether or not Wolsey pur-

> "A great carl he is and fat
> Wearing on his head a red hat."
> *A popular ballad critical of Cardinal Wolsey.*

Above The Battle of Pavia, 1525. A detail from a contemporary Flemish painting.

sued a policy which could one day give him the Papacy, there is no denying that this is what he craved. Even at the Field of Cloth of Gold he thought that the Emperor's friendship would give him a better chance.

As a result, he had encouraged Henry and the Emperor Charles V to sign a treaty of common cause against France in 1520. In 1525 at the Battle of Pavia France had been crushed by Charles V's army. This had been Henry's chance to march on Paris and claim the throne of France. However, Charles V did not see why England should gain so much for contributing nothing to his victory. Thwarted and in a petty spite, Wolsey tried to arrange a combination of France, England and the Pope against the Emperor. It came to nothing. Nothing, apparently, could stop Charles now and in 1527 his troops marched into Rome and virtually held the Pope a prisoner. Charles now controlled most of Europe. Wolsey's aim of keeping a balance of power in Europe lay in ruins. From the dizzy moments of 1518, when all Europe looked to London, England had slumped, a nonentity by 1527 in a Europe dominated by the victorious Emperor.

Wolsey's failure made Henry VIII angry. Squeezing money to pay for his ambitious foreign policy made Wolsey hated by most Englishmen. It had been very expensive indeed. In the past few years Henry had squandered most of the royal fortune left to him by his father. Between his accession and June 1513 Henry had spent more than £1,000,000, some two-thirds of it to pay for the war with France. In normal times, if the King did not indulge in costly foreign wars, he could live comfortably off his own income. This came from two main sources, his land, and customs duties. The King was a great landowner; the rents and profits were collected by his officials up and down the country and paid into the Royal Exchequer. When this was not enough, the King was forced to raise extra taxes. For this the permission of Parliament had to be obtained. Parliament was therefore a powerful organ of government; yet it only existed when the King chose to summon it. He could dissolve it or prorogue (suspend) it at any time. It always met in his presence, and whatever Parliament decided could only become law after the King had given his royal assent.

By 1523 Henry was forced to summon Parliament to ask for more money. He sent as his representative Lord Chancellor Wolsey. Wolsey was always awkward when facing Parliament and all his diplomatic skill, so successful when talking to foreign diplomats, was wasted on the massed representatives of the English towns and counties. They listened to his arguments and then for four months argued over his requests for a levy of 4 shillings in the pound. After lengthy debate they agreed to levy a tax of 2 shillings in the pound.

In the next year yet more money was needed. This time Wolsey was determined to go it alone without Parliament. He sent out officers to collect a levy on all men of property. This was called rather optimistically an Amicable Grant. It was the last straw. There were signs of open rebellion in East Anglia and Kent. At this moment the King stepped in, and claiming that he knew nothing about the Amicable Grant cancelled it at once.

This action made Henry doubly popular and his minister disliked even more. Henry had implied that Wolsey was acting without his knowledge, and that the money was lining Wolsey's own pockets. This was quite untrue, but Wolsey as the scapegoat was certainly the most hated man in England.

Wolsey's continuance in office depended solely on the King's support. This would only last if Wolsey could give the King what he wanted. When Henry asked Wolsey to begin negotiations about divorcing Catherine Wolsey tried desperately hard to talk him out of it. Wolsey could only see disaster ahead. The Pope would never grant a divorce. He was a prisoner of the Emperor in Rome, and was not the Emperor the nephew of Queen Catherine? He would never let the Pope disgrace the name of his family and that of his aunt.

Below Windsor Castle, from a descriptive painting of the sixteenth century. Henry was a very rich king, and Windsor is an example of his many elaborate country palaces.

8 The King's Great Matter

SOMETIME IN the years 1525–6 the human element got mixed up with the theological and political. Henry happened to catch sight of one of Queen Catherine's ladies-in-waiting, Anne Boleyn, and fell earnestly and passionately in love with her. Anne was not particularly beautiful. True, she had raven black hair and black almond-shaped eyes. But most people thought she had too long a neck and that her complexion was too sallow. Her enemies liked to whisper about the sixth finger on her left hand. This deformity she skilfully concealed, but was it not a sure sign of witchcraft and sorcery?

Henry was certainly bewitched. Anne transformed him. The Boleyns were quite an influential family of merchants in the City of London. On her mother's side she was related to the Duke of Norfolk. Anne had not been the first Boleyn to attract the King's attention. Some years before, her sister Mary had been Henry's mistress. Indeed Anne owed her position at court to Mary's influence.

Anne was determined not to be just another Bessie Blount, or be like her sister—enjoying the King's company for a few years, bearing him a child, only to be discarded. Nothing less than Queen of England was good enough for Anne. This determination not to yield to the King's advances probably explains his infatuation. He was used to getting his own way. The harder Anne made it, the more infatuated Henry became.

Henry had never been a great letter writer, but now in a burst of passion the pages poured forth. He complained of being separated from Anne and longed to be with her again. In 1528 they were apart for some time, for this was the year of the plague or "sweating

> "Mademoiselle Boleyn has come to the court at London and the King has set her in a very fine lodging, which he has furnished very near his own. Greater court is paid to her every day than has been for a long time paid to the Queen." *Cardinal Du Bellay, French Ambassador in London (December 1528).*

sickness". For all his bravura and heartiness the King was terrified of sickness. At the first sign of plague he would escape from the crowded city of London to the purer air of one of his country palaces. The "sweating sickness" was a terrifying disease, as he wrote in one of his letters to Anne. "One has a little pain in the heart and head," he wrote. "Suddenly a sweat breaks out and a physician is useless, for whether you wrap yourself little or much in four hours, sometimes in two or three, you are despatched without languishing." That summer he felt very much alone "wishing myself specially on an

Above Henry with Anne Boleyn. An engraving from the painting by William Hogarth.

Above Anne Boleyn, second wife of Henry VIII.

evening in my sweet hearts arms, whose pretty dukkys I trust shortly to kiss."

The more Anne insisted on marriage the more did Henry agree that she must become the rightful Queen and mother of England's heir. If Henry was to do what both his mind and heart dictated, the only way was by divorce.

When Anne and Henry fell in love, little did they realize that not until 1533 would their love be consummated and they be made man and wife. The wrangle of Henry's divorce was to be a long and tedious one.

For any divorce to be legal the Church had to give its blessing. This the Pope was reluctant to do in Henry's case: as we have seen, Rome was under the control of Charles V, Catherine's nephew. When at last the news was broken to Catherine in June 1527 of Henry's plans she appealed to her nephew. Charles V at once rallied to her cause and called on both Henry and the Pope to drop the idea. In the circumstances the Pope would hardly let the divorce go through.

At first negotiations were kept very secret. These got nowhere and Henry tried to take matters into his own hands. But it was no good. At length Wolsey did persuade the Pope to allow an open hearing in London, and to send a special representative, Cardinal Lorenzo Campeggio. Campeggio was a gouty old man who took four months to get to London from Rome. Campeggio was under direct orders from the Pope to play for time and not to upset Charles. Before the actual hearing began he tried to reconcile Catherine and Henry. Henry utterly refused to co-operate. For the first time he exclaimed in public that if things went wrong he would desert Rome for Lutheranism.

Campeggio's next delaying tactic was to try and coax Catherine into a nunnery. At first she quite liked the idea but in the end she said "no"—unless Henry became a monk! Meantime the legal arguments and counter-arguments dragged on. Campeggio himself was taken ill. Not until June 1529, some eight months after his arrival, did the hearing actually open at Blackfriars in

London.

Public opinion in the meantime was growing in favour of Queen Catherine. Cardinal Campeggio himself was jostled in the streets with cries of "No Nan Boleyn for us!" Queen Catherine, said one courtier, was "beloved as if she had been of the blood royal of England." Henry, always conscious of his public image, decided to do something about it. In November 1528 he called together a representative collection of nobles, judges and leading merchants to explain "the woes that trouble my mind—the pangs that trouble my conscience." Henry said that if the clerks studying the case could only prove that Catherine was his legal wife—despite her earlier marriage to Prince Arthur—he would gladly marry her again. All this talk did not really impress anyone. Henry obviously wanted a new wife who could bear him a son.

The stock of Catherine's support grew even larger when the official legatine court finally opened on 18th June 1529. This had in the person of Cardinal Campeggio the full authority of the Pope to try the case and reach a decision. At the beginning of the tribunal Catherine herself appeared in person. When Henry came into the court, she rushed to him, brushing aside all decorum, and fell to her knees. She begged him not to dishonour her or her daughter Mary. Becoming more and more emotional she cried out to Henry, "When ye first had me I was a true maid!" Henry remained unmoved through this tirade. Catherine openly challenged the court to accuse her of being Prince Arthur's wife and therefore wrongfully married to Henry. If so, she would gladly "depart to my great shame and honour." With these words in defence of her family honour and Hapsburg pride she swept out of the chamber to brood alone in her apartments. She never returned to the courtroom.

Catherine had refused to accept the court's jurisdiction and instead appealed directly to the Pope in Rome. The court continued to sit. Bishop Fisher of Rochester spoke vehemently on her behalf, but without Catherine

Above Cardinal Lorenzo Campeggio, the legate of the Pope, who came to England to try the divorce case between Henry and Catherine of Aragon. Instead he tried to put off the hearing by attempting to reconcile the two.

"For of necessity I must ensure me of this answer, having been now above one whole year struck with the dart of love, not being assured either of failure, or of finding place in your heart and grounded affection.... If it shall please you to do me the office of a true loyal mistress and friend, and to give yourself up, body and soul, to me ... I will take you for my only mistress, rejecting from thought and affection all others save yourself, to serve you only." *A love letter from Henry VIII to Anne Boleyn (1527).*

> "But if I had served God as diligently as I have done the King, he would not have given me over in my grey hairs. Howbeit this is the just reward that I must receive for my worldly diligence and pains that I have had to do him service, only to satisfy his vain pleasures, not regarding my godly deity. Wherefore I pray you with all my heart to have me most humbly commended unto his royal majesty, beseeking him in my behalf to call to his most gracious remembrance all matters proceeding between him and me from the beginning of the world unto this day." *Some of the reputed last words of Cardinal Wolsey. (George Cavendish, "Life and Death of Cardinal Wolsey").*

Below Cardinal Wolsey, from a contemporary woodcut.

in person it was indecisive. By the end of July 1529, Cardinal Campeggio declared the court adjourned. Henry was furious but for all his bad temper he was powerless. He did his best to spite Catherine who was by now so popular everywhere. She was sent packing and refused permission ever to see her daughter Mary. As a final insult, Anne Boleyn moved into Catherine's apartments.

The court of Campeggio did not meet again. Papal messengers arrived in the summer of 1529 referring the whole case to Rome. Henry would have to go in person to plead before the Pope. He felt humiliated before his own subjects and in the eyes of Europe. It made up his mind. He could not, would not, go. How could the King of England crawl on his knees to a Pope who was little more than a pawn at the mercy of imperial troops in the capital? No, he would stay in England. The King of England must decide his own destiny.

The decision of venue of the divorce proceedings had virtually decided the fate of the links between the Pope and the King of England. It had also decided the fate of Wolsey. Wolsey had served the King well in the past. But Henry was never a man to let sentimentality get the better of him. If someone had outrun their usefulness he would not hesitate to strike them down. Wolsey had not managed to obtain the divorce and he would have to go.

The blow fell swiftly in September 1529. Wolsey was asked to lay down his seals of office as Lord Chancellor. A virtual outcast, he went up to York to pay his first visit to the city of which he had been Archbishop for fifteen years. At the end of November 1530 he was summoned back to London to face charges of treason. In a desperate bid to win back favour he had tried privately to reopen proceedings over the divorce. He had been corresponding with Rome to this effect. To Henry this was enough to bring about Wolsey's end; how dare he negotiate secretly with a foreign power! On 29th November 1530, on his way to face certain execution, this gigantic figure of a man who had lived like a king died at Leicester Abbey of a broken heart and in abject misery.

9 The Break with Rome

BY 1530 Henry VIII had ruled for 21 years. His reign so far had accomplished little. He had lived vainly, gloriously and extravagantly. He had spent all his fortunes on idle pleasure and a profitless European war. He had delegated to Wolsey most of the affairs of state and England's policy in turn had been shaped to Wolsey's ambition. The actual means of government had not changed since his father's day.

The riotous living, the hunting, the dancing and banqueting, and above all the recent worry over the divorce and the desperate need for a son and heir, had all left their mark. By 1530 Henry was no longer the handsome young lion of former years; he was definitely putting on weight. He still loved to play tennis but the feet that once danced around the court were sluggish and his physical demeanour rather clumsy and undignified.

He still enjoyed hunting and riding, but two accidents had dimmed his enthusiasm. In March 1524, while riding in the lists with his brother-in-law the Duke of Suffolk, he had forgotten to lower his visor. The crowd saw his mistake and shouted to warn him. Henry thought their shouts were those of encouragement to ride faster. He rode straight into Suffolk's lance, which shattered against his helmet and splintered in his face. He could easily have been killed or injured, and was lucky to escape with minor bruises.

A year later he was out hunting on foot near Hitchin in Hertfordshire. Coming to a ditch he tried to vault over it using his pole. But the pole broke and Henry landed head-first in a river of mud. Such was his weight and the awkwardness of his fall that he was unable to

Below An engraving of the portrait of Henry by Hans Holbein.

Above Henry in armour and mounted for the joust.

move. He might have drowned if someone had not been near to pull him out of danger. It was comical to see the King's legs frantically kicking the air and his huge body stuck head first in the mud. But it proved, yet again, how near the heirless King had been to death, and was a very unnerving experience.

Henry was afraid of death. Perhaps it was because it would have meant anarchy in the kingdom; perhaps it was just the fear of a man who enjoyed life too much to let it go. He was very afraid of illness, too. In 1514 he had been laid low with smallpox. In 1521 he had suffered a bout of malaria after a mosquito bite. In 1528 an ulcer appeared in one leg and quickly spread to the other. In the end this immobilized him. The young King who had been the very model of youth and high spirits was already showing signs of the advance of age and ill-health and with it increasing worry, corpulence and bad temper.

Worry and temper were, however, no answer to his problem. Henry was still married to Catherine of Aragon and Anne Boleyn was becoming impatient in the wings. As early as 1529 Henry had told the Emperor's ambassador in London that the Pope's power in England was very limited, and suggested that he himself might take over the finances and running of the Church in England if help on the divorce was not forthcoming. After all, why should he not be both head of the state and head of the Church? This idea was novel and revolutionary in the sixteenth century. Emperors before Henry had tried to exercise rights over the Church but in the end they had always been forced to acknowledge the supremacy of the Pope in spiritual affairs. Henry was determined that if the Pope went on being obstinate, he would appoint himself head of the Church in England and grant his own divorce.

The Church in England and its clergy were a very powerful, very influential body. Religion dominated much of people's daily lives. Overseas visitors often commented on the number of services which took place each day, and the endless ringing of bells to call the people to church. Churches were still being built; Bath Abbey and extensions at Fountains Abbey were notable examples.

Yet for all this the clergy were unpopular. The peasantry had a special grievance against the tithe (tenth) they had to pay to the Church on their tiny incomes. As they struggled to make ends meet they observed the swelling riches of the Church and its worldly-wise ministers. A "pluralist" vicar might hold two or three livings with a large salary and not even bother to turn up to the services. Cardinal Wolsey's son held thirteen ecclesiastical posts all at the same time while still a schoolboy.

These scandals about the clergy might have mattered less if they had been fewer in number. There was one clergyman for every 50–100 of the population. The clergy collected about a tenth of the national income and owned a quarter of the land in England. In addition they held most of the top positions in the country. They also had their own private system of ecclesiastical courts and were exempt from the ordinary courts of justice. This was not so with the laity. They could be fined by both courts for many offences. Also, justice seemed to be on the side of the clergy. If a clergyman was accused of fathering a bastard he would be fined five shillings (25p). A member of his congregation accused of a similar offence could be fined £2.

The clergy were a powerful group of people. They could control life in their locality. For instance they could close down butchers' shops in Lent and on other fast days. Everyone had to go to confession and take Holy Communion at least once a year, or risk excommunication. From the pulpit the clergy could deliver subtle yet powerful propaganda. The clergyman was a powerful if mistrusted figure.

As we have seen, Henry VIII only called Parliament when he wanted financial rescue. With all other avenues exhausted, Parliament must now help him divorce Catherine. In this hope he was lucky. The new Parliament that met on 3rd November 1529 well represented the feeling that the Church needed reforming and its

Above Bath Abbey, built during the reign of Henry VIII. The Abbey was a result of the upsurge of religious interest at the time when Henry decided to become head of the Church in England, as well as of the State.

THE CARELESSE NON-RESIDENT

Above A cartoon criticizing the practice, common during Henry's reign, of "absentee" priests. These priests obtained "livings" (sources of wealth) in a number of different parishes. They never, or only seldom, appeared in the parishes to preach or care for the parishioners, but accepted the parish dues, adding them to their private income. (The cartoon is from a later period).

"We your most humble subjects, daily orators and bedesmen of your clergy of England, having our special trust and confidence in your most exalted wisdom.... First do offer and promise ... here unto your highness, submitting ourselves most humbly to the same, that we will never from henceforth presume to attempt, allege, claim or yet put in use, or to enact ... constitution or ordinance provincial ... unless your highness by royal assent shall license us to make, promulgate and execute the same, and thereto give your most royal assent and authority." *The opening of the Submission of the Clergy, 15th May 1532.*

clergy's power curtailing. It has been suggested that this Parliament was "packed" by Henry to give him an overwhelming majority. There was certainly a minority, led by the new Lord Chancellor, Sir Thomas More, who were against him. But More's was a lone voice. The assembled M.P.s were only too pleased to hear Henry's complaint about the Pope and help him sever the links with Rome.

At first the "Reformation" Parliament, as it is called, concerned itself with fairly minor matters. But in December 1530, Henry struck his first real blow against the clergy. He accused the whole of the English clergy of a breach of *praemunire* (virtually an act of treason) because they had falsely recognized Wolsey as the Pope's representative in England. They were fined £100,000 and ordered to recognize Henry as "their singular protector and supreme Lord".

Two years later Henry moved against them again. On 11th May 1532 he addressed the Speaker and a dozen members of the House of Commons. He said he had just discovered that the clergy "be but half our subjects, yea and scarce our subjects." In other words the clergy were more likely to obey the dictates of the Pope in Rome than those of the King of England. On 15th May Convocation, the assembly of clergymen, made its surrender or "submission of the clergy". In future all matters regarding the Church needed the King's agreement before the clergy could act. This was too much for Lord Chancellor More. Hearing of their submission he resigned his ancient seals of office, wanting no more to serve a King who seemed bent on destroying the Church he loved.

For all his new-felt power Henry was still married to Catherine of Aragon and the divorce seemed no nearer. Anne had by 1532 been waiting for six years. Henry tried his best to keep her happy. To appease her he created her Marquess of Pembroke with lands worth £1,000 a year.

Events after all this delay now began to move quickly. After ensuring that Francis I of France would not oppose him Henry decided to go it alone. In August 1532, the old Archbishop of Canterbury William Warham (1450?–1532) died. Here was a chance to appoint someone of his own choice. A shy, quiet, learned man, Thomas Cranmer (1489–1556), had come into prominence a few years earlier when he had suggested that Henry might test opinion in the universities of Europe as to whether they believed his divorce was permissible or not. This idea had come to nothing, but Henry liked Cranmer and wished to appoint him as the next Archbishop.

This chance of a sympathetic archbishop seemed to bring Henry and Anne Boleyn's marriage a little closer. Early in September 1532, Anne and Henry probably began to live together as man and wife. At Christmas or early in the New Year they were secretly married by an unknown cleric. By mid-January Anne was pregnant. Although Henry had to move fast this piece of news was concealed until the Pope had confirmed Thomas Cranmer as the next Archbishop. Within a few hours of this being known in London, Anne Boleyn told one of her former lovers "that for three days she had such a violent desire to eat apples as she had never felt before, and that the King told her she must be with child." At

"Squire Henry means to be God and do as he pleases." *Martin Luther.*

"Henry has rare endowments both of mind and of body, such as personal beauty, genius, learning etc, and it is marvellous how he has fallen into so many errors and false tenets." *Carlo Capello, a Catholic's opinion of Henry's divorce proceedings.*

Left The private marriage of Henry to Anne Boleyn.

Above Thomas Cranmer, from the painting of 1546 by Gerlach Flicke.

last the news was out. The gossip that had filled the court these many months was confirmed.

On 9th April 1533, Catherine was informed she was no longer Queen. Under virtual house arrest at Ampthill she was told that the King had taken another wife and that from now on she would be called the Princess Dowager. A month later a tribunal led by the new Archbishop declared that Henry and Catherine had never legally been man and wife, and that the marriage between Anne and Henry was therefore valid.

On the 31st May 1533, to make up for her secret wedding, Anne was afforded a magnificent coronation. To allow for her pregnant figure an extra panel was fitted to her skirts and her long black hair flowed down so long that "she could sit upon it in her litter." A flotilla of three hundred barges accompanied her as she sailed in state down the River Thames to Westminster Abbey. In the Abbey, Archbishop Cranmer placed St. Edward's crown on her head and anointed her with holy oil. Anne Boleyn had achieved her avowed ambition to be crowned as England's Queen.

The splendours of the procession and of the scene in Westminster Abbey itself were offset by the lukewarm reception given to Anne by the London crowd. Plenty of wine flowed in the streets but there was no real rejoicing. Despite her triumph Anne had failed to win the hearts of the people. One man was heard to cry out, "God save Queen Catherine, our own righteous Queen!" Another called out to Anne, "Goggle-eyed whore!" Apprentice boys in the streets made great play with the initials "H.A." that were emblazoned everywhere. "Ha! Ha!" they shouted in mock contempt at their new Queen.

At Anne's coronation Henry had taken a back seat. But really it was his triumph. He was King of England as there had never been a King before; he now had control over the Church and State. His subjects never much liked the later religious changes which this entailed, but they realized that Henry had acted principally to give England a male heir. For this he had their grudging consent. Everyone waited in hope.

10 Henry Feels his Strength

HENRY AND HIS SUBJECTS had not long to wait. On 7th September 1533 Queen Anne gave birth to a baby girl, Princess Elizabeth. If Henry could have foreseen the future glories of his daughter's reign he would not have been disappointed. But it was not so. We can understand his feelings when, after six long years of argument, and years of soul-searching over the validity of his original marriage to Catherine, he was presented with another baby girl.

But we cannot excuse his conduct. Henry adamantly refused to go to the christening. Instead of a joyful atmosphere at court and in the streets, everything to do with the christening was "very cold and disagreeable." No bonfires were lit. With little regard to the mother's or baby's feelings Henry established a separate household for the new princess; here she was taken early in December 1533 to be looked after by the ladies of the court.

After several weeks in low spirits, Henry began to cheer up a little. After all Queen Catherine had entered one pregnancy after another; surely Anne could, too. There could still be boys.

Meantime, the birth of a girl did not help the King's popularity. To a man of Henry's belief and to a superstitious nation used to look for signs of God's anger or pleasure in the weather, the birth of a girl could only mean one thing—the marriage lacked divine approval. A simple nun from Canterbury, Elizabeth Barton ("the Holy Maid of Kent") had prophesied dire things if Henry ever divorced Catherine. He would cease to be King within a month and he would die a villain's death. Elizabeth Barton soon became the rallying point

> "Where by diverse, sundry, old, authentic histories and chronicles it is manifestly declared and explained that this realm of England is an empire, and so hath been accepted in the world, governed by one supreme head and King, having the dignity and royal estate of the 'imperial crown' of the same, unto whom a body politic, compact of all sorts and degrees of people divided in terms and by names of spirituality and temporality, be bounden and owe next to God a natural and humble obedience." *The skilful preamble to the Act in Restraint of Appeals (1533) which sets out to prove the powers Henry was assuming were not revolutionary but in the English tradition.*

Above John Fisher, Bishop of Rochester, one of the chief opponents to the divorce of Henry and Catherine of Aragon.

of those who did not like the King to tamper with the old religion. Now that Queen Anne had produced a daughter Henry thought the Maid's presence too dangerous. She might have a following as wide and influential as that other famous mystic, Joan of Arc, the Maid of Orleans. Henry was impatient, and as big men in tight corners often do he hit back.

The Maid of Kent was brought to London, and on 23rd November 1533 she and her leading followers were stood on a platform erected before the steps of St. Paul's Cathedral. They were subjected to open ridicule and humiliation. John Salcot, the Abbot of Hyde, preached a long sermon and denounced the nun as a harlot, a fraud, one who had fallen victim to her own vanity. Soon after she was arrested on charges of high treason and in April next year was hanged at Tyburn (where Marble Arch now stands) along with four associates.

Two other men, Bishop Fisher of Rochester and Sir Thomas More, were living dangerously. Both were in the Tower of London for refusing to agree to Catherine's divorce or to recognize Anne as Henry's rightful wife. Fisher was a saintly, scholarly man, adamant in Catherine's defence. When Pope Paul III (1534–49) made Fisher a Cardinal it might have been his death warrant. Henry was angry to think that Fisher had the Pope's support. Fisher could easily become the focus of a rebellion. His head must roll. On 22nd June 1535 he was executed.

Likewise with Sir Thomas More. The self-appointed champion of learning and literature, Henry was about to kill the one man in England who more than any other represented the forward-looking Renaissance spirit. In those far off happy days when the young King called on More at his home in Chelsea, the King would walk around his garden joking and laughing, his arm around More's shoulders. Even then More understood only too well the King's volatile nature. Afterwards he commented, "If my head could win him a castle in France it should not fail to go." The head of the one genius in England was now to go. Some two weeks after Fisher's

Left Thomas More, his family and his descendants, a composite group by an unknown artist. Left to right: Sir John More, father of Sir Thomas; Anne Cressacre, daughter-in-law of Sir Thomas; Sir Thomas More; his son John More II; Sir Thomas's three daughters, Cecily Heron, Elizabeth Dauncey, and Margaret Roper; John More III, great grandson of Sir Thomas.

execution (6th July 1535) Thomas More faced his own death by the axe on Tower Hill. Henry was beginning to feel his strength and would not be thwarted in his royal designs. As Sir Thomas More had once said of Henry, "If a lion knew his strength it were hard for any man to rule him."

One man at least seemed able to influence the King—Thomas Cromwell (1485?–1540). Cromwell is the dominant person in the second half of Henry's reign as Wolsey is for the first. Born of a humble family in Putney, his father had been a small businessman. Thomas's earliest experience in the world had been as a mercenary soldier in Italy. This was undoubtedly a baptism of fire, a worldly training which would well equip him to survive in the cut and thrust of Henry's court. After Italy Thomas set up as a merchant with connections in Antwerp and London. He was largely self-educated but had been able to grasp several languages. Being ambitious he joined Cardinal Wolsey's household and became his lawyer. Here his obvious efficiency and ability marked him out, and when Wolsey was disgraced

"He likes to dress simply, and does not wear silk or purple or gold chains. . . . In social intercourse he is of so rare a courtesy and charm of manners that there is no man so melancholy that he does not gladden, no subject so forbidding that he does not dispel the tedium of it." *From Erasmus's description of Sir Thomas More.*

"Pluck up thy spirit, man, and be not afraid to do thy office, my neck is very short: take heed therefore that thou strike not away, for saving of thy honesty." *Sir Thomas More to his executioner. Roper's "Life of Thomas More."*

Above Thomas Cromwell.

Cromwell was promoted into the King's own service. His rise to prominence is obscure but rapid. He came to the King's attention in the difficult year of 1532. Next year he became the king's chief minister and in 1534 his principal secretary.

Cromwell has always had a bad press. Historians have written of him as an evil and ambitious man. Yet he never liked display and always lived humbly; it is to Cromwell that we owe the eventual emergence of a modern system of government. It was he who followed through Henry's idea of getting a divorce into a complete break with Rome.

Cromwell was in charge of the Parliament that so readily agreed to the transfer of power from Rome to Henry. This could be done quickly, and without too much hostility, because most English people were dissatisfied with the over-privileged place of the clergy in society. People were content to witness and endorse the acts that made them more an equal part of society. Cromwell actually pushed the King further than he really wanted to go. The legislation which followed in 1534 culminated in the Act of Supremacy, giving Henry total control of the Church. This, with the Act of Succession which made Henry's offspring with Anne the rightful heirs to the throne, gave him unprecedented power.

As Henry trod unexplored ground in his break with Rome he wanted to feel quite sure that his subjects supported him. The whole nation had to swear an oath to uphold the Acts of Supremacy and Succession. They were asked to act as never before as a united nation. At their head stood a truly nationalistic monarch, directing England's affairs with almost divine authority. Even if most Englishmen were dismayed at seeing Queen Catherine cast aside and the old religion threatened, they would always hold back from rebellion. They felt that Henry acted for them and in their own interests, even if they sometimes failed to grasp their full significance. To destroy Henry would in a way destroy England and perhaps open again the floodgates of anarchy of a century before.

11 One Queen after Another

HENRY HAD STRUCK out with death against those who stood in his way. Now death was to claim another victim. On 7th January 1536 Catherine died. There were rumours that she had been poisoned, but far more likely it was the result of the last few years—the neglect, scorn and abuse she had suffered during the divorce crisis and in her lonely existence afterwards. When news reached London of her death Henry and Anne callously celebrated it with dancing, jousting and feasting. Both dressed in bright yellow to show their delight at the news. As one of Henry's biographers has remarked, "He was every inch a King, but never a gentleman."

With Catherine's death the divorce proceedings now seemed quite unnecessary. Henry had for some time been feeling frustrated and fed up with Anne Boleyn. Catherine had been a dutiful and meek wife. Anne was the opposite. Henry was asserting his power and influence in the country but he was often put in his place by his wife. If Anne could produce the male heir he so desperately wanted she might make herself secure. But on 29th January 1536, within weeks of the celebration ball at the news of Catherine's death, Anne had a miscarriage. This settled her fate. It looked like a repetition of Queen Catherine's misfortunes all over again.

The excuse which Anne gave for this mishap was the shock she had on hearing that Henry had fallen from his horse. Indeed, this had been very serious. While Henry had been riding in heavy armour an opponent had unhorsed him and, as he fell, the horse fell on top of him. For two hours he lay unconscious and his life seemed in danger.

Henry never rode again. This accident may have been

> "Anne was becoming more arrogant every day, using words and authority towards the King of which he has several times complained to the Duke of Norfolk, saying that she was not like the Queen Catherine who never in her life used ill words to him." *Chapuys, Spanish Ambassador.*

Above Henry VIII, from the portrait by Hans Holbein. Compare this treatment of Holbein's painting with that on page 45.

the cause of much of his pain. The King became more and more susceptible to severe pain in the legs caused by ulcers. It used to be said that the King's disease was syphilis but this has been more or less ruled out by modern research. The explanation most often given nowadays is osteomyelitis. This is just as unpleasant as varicose ulcers. After such a fall as Henry's the thigh bone could quite easily have become infected. Puss is discharged intermittently and pieces of splintered bone can work their way through to the surface of the skin. Pain with this disease is punctuated by long intervals of comparative comfort. This may well explain Henry's increasing unpredictability and bouts of violent temper.

Recovering from his accident, and not feeling in the best of health or temper, Henry began to ponder the best way to rid himself of Anne. In truth he had begun to fall out of love with her as soon as Princess Elizabeth had been born. Brooding over his lot and thinking how he had been captivated into loving and eventually marrying her it seemed as if those black eyes and long black hair had really "bewitched" him. But he needed more substantial charges than these.

As Henry had once been eager to marry her, so now he was eager to cast her aside. In the September following Elizabeth's birth Henry had fallen in love with Jane Seymour (1509–37). Jane Seymour was shy, and refused the King's advances. This, of course, only made Henry even more interested. It was much like old times with the King bursting with a frenzy of passion. The only difference now was that with Anne it had been a game; with Jane it was a more serious matter. Jane was even-tempered and "full of goodness, of middle stature and no great beauty."

The prospect of Jane was very tempting, but how to get rid of Queen Anne? Eventually charges of adultery were brought against her including a case of incest with her brother Lord Rochford. The actual charges may have been trumped up, but there was always a question mark about Anne. Certainly the tone of the court had grown much more lax since her arrival. Indeed, one am-

"And the morrow after... at two o'clock in the morning the Queen was delivered of a man child. And the same day, at eight of the clock in the morning, Te Deum was sung in every parish church throughout London, with all the bells ringing in every church and great fires made in every street.... Also the same night... there was new fires made in every street, people sitting at them banqueting with fruits and wine and hogsheads of wine set in divers places of the city for poor people to drink as long as they liked; the mayor and aldermen riding about the city thanking the people, and praying them to give laud and praise to God for our Prince." *Wriothesley writing in his "Chronicle" on the birth of Prince Edward.*

Left Jane Seymour, third wife of Henry VIII. From the portrait by Hans Holbein.

bassador was surprised to learn that Jane Seymour was still a virgin who "had been so long at court."

Anne's "amorous adventures" were in Henry's eyes high treason. Treason meant death and the King in a spiteful rage demanded the ultimate penalty. Having been found guilty Anne was beheaded on Tower Hill on

> "On a scaffold made there for the said execution the said Queen Anne said thus: Masters I here humbly submit me to the law as the law hath judged me... beseeching God to have mercy on my soul, and I beseech Jesu save my sovereign and master the King, the most godly, noble and gentle Prince that is, and long to reign over you: which words were spoken with a goodly smiling countenance; and this done, she kneeled down on her knees and said: To Jesus Christ I commend my soul; and suddenly the hangman cut off her head at a stroke with a sword."
> Wriothesley's "Chronicle."

Below Edward, first son of Henry VIII. He became Edward VI, King of England from 1547 to 1553.

19th May 1536. There were no brave speeches from her, but she conducted herself with quiet dignity. She put on a simple robe of grey damask, cut low and trimmed with fur. To make it easy for her executioner she wore her long black hair tucked up under a net with a head-dress embroidered with pearls. The night before her execution she had tried to joke with her jailer. She had put her hands round her "little neck", saying it would not be difficult for the executioner. The one luxury Henry afforded to Anne was to bring over an expert swordsman from St. Omer in France. The man obliged Anne by cutting off her head in one clean stroke.

This time Henry did not dress up in yellow, though he did act with unseemly indiscretion. The very next day he went to see Jane Seymour and became engaged to her. Within a month of Anne's execution they were married.

In addition to her charm and modesty, what attracted Henry to Jane was the Seymour family tree. It had been particularly fruitful, and produced a healthy crop of boys. The worry of having no male heir was still uppermost in Henry's mind. He was now over forty and in sixteenth-century terms fast approaching old age. The new Act of Succession passed in 1536 made this obvious. This cancelled the Act passed after the Boleyn marriage. It recognized the legality of the new marriage and declared that both Princess Mary and Princess Elizabeth were illegitimate. Since there was no legal heir to the throne it gave Henry the right to nominate his successor.

Then, one day, all the clouds lifted from the sky. All the worry about the future and the doubts and misgivings of the past suddenly vanished when on 12th October 1537 Queen Jane gave birth to a boy—Edward (King of England 1547–53). Poor Jane did not live to enjoy her triumph. Tudor medicine was crude and inefficient and twelve days after the birth she died of puerperal fever. Henry's grief was massive and sincere. Jane's body lay in state for three weeks before being buried amidst great pomp in St. George's Chapel, Windsor. The mother was dead, but the little boy grew and prospered. This was Henry's finest hour.

12 Newfound Riches

BY THE MID-1530S Henry was once again desperately short of money. The Reformation Parliament which had given him so much power had avoided granting him money. True, Henry had steered clear of war for several years now, but England still had to be defended and this cost a good deal of money. In 1533 the defence of the Scottish border cost nearly £25,000 and the suppression of an Irish rebellion in 1534 another £36,000. In addition the life of the court became ever more extravagant, ever more taxing on the depleted royal coffers. Cash would have to come from somewhere. To Thomas Cromwell it became a matter of some urgency to relieve Henry's embarrassment and it soon became uncomfortably clear that the only way out of this financial mess was to take money from the Church.

There can be no doubt that the main motive for investigating and then dissolving the monasteries was financial. Land in the sixteenth century was owned by few people. The King was the single biggest landowner, but far and away the next biggest share of land was owned by the Church. In 1530 there were some 825 monasteries in England and between them they owned between a fifth and a quarter of the total landed wealth of the country. For a long time Henry had been casting covetous eyes on the Church's wealth. Cromwell talked of making Henry "the richest that ever was in England" and Cromwell it was who was appointed by Henry, as Vicar-General, to lead the investigations into the monasteries' resources and prepare the way for their eventual dissolution.

> "And so with as fair words as we could, we have conveyed him [the Abbot] to the tower ... but now the abbot being gone, we will, with as much celerity as we may, proceed to the despatching of the monks. We have in money £300 and above .... also we have found a fair chalice of gold, and divers other parcels of plate, which the abbot had hid secretly from all such commissioners as have been there in times past." *A letter from Cromwell's agents after a visit to Glastonbury Abbey, September 1539.*

The noble ideals of a strict religious life, devoted to prayer or community service, had made the monastic way of life a potent force in the middle ages. But by the 1530s this had been frittered away to almost nothing. Ironically, the very ease with which the monks gave up the struggle showed how these ideals had lost their vigour. Less than 5 per cent of the monasteries' vast wealth went to help the poor and needy. Few of the monasteries were truly charitable. Most of them spent more on entertaining the local gentry or visiting dignitaries than on the deserving poor.

Cromwell's visitors toured the monasteries in the winter of 1534–5 to make an inventory of all their property. They found plenty of evidence to back up the King's suspicions of their laxity. The eventual survey *Valor Ecclesiasticus* (Church Wealth) contained the evidence that Cromwell needed to press before Parliament the urgent need to dissolve the monasteries. First it was the turn of the smaller houses; in the early months of 1536 Parliament passed an act dissolving all monasteries with an annual income of less than £200. This was the start. During the next few years larger abbeys came under the grip of Cromwell's visitors.

By annexing the wealth of the monasteries for himself Henry received land worth more than £100,000 a year. Skilfully he made this new income even greater —possibly as high as £1,500,000—by selling or leasing out these great estates. Not only did he increase his wealth, but by handing out the land in this way he purchased loyalty to the Tudor dynasty and to the course of the Reformation.

The Reformation or change in religion which affected everyone's lives was no easy thing to accomplish. Henry could cut off as many Queens' heads as he liked; this was something which left ordinary folk unmoved. But when he started to interfere with people's private lives it was a different matter. With the redistribution of monastic land every tenant farmer in England had a new landlord. Also the monastery buildings, so much a part of village life for centuries, were now mostly pulled down.

Religious worship was more or less unchanged, but by 1536 Henry VIII seemed to have moved closer towards Protestantism. The Ten Acts of that year, an open compromise between Protestantism and Catholicism, were seen by most Catholics as a warning beacon for worse to come. The old Catholic beliefs in good works and beautiful images and prayers for the dead were included; but only three of the traditional seven sacraments were mentioned—baptism, penance and forgiveness. The most revolutionary suggestion was that the Bible should be translated from Latin into English. The average Englishman was conservative when he thought his religion was under attack. When he could see the monasteries being destroyed, and feel the inflation of the 1530s which was blamed on Henry's religious policy, he became actively resentful and distrustful.

The mid-1530s proved to be the toughest years of Henry's reign. When news reached Sussex of the King's

Above The dissolution of the monasteries, from a picture entitled "Vandals of the Reformation". The Reformation was the period which began when Henry took away the wealth of the Church for himself and for his nobles. It was a prelude to the establishment of Protestantism in England.

bad fall that had caused Anne to have a miscarriage, one man said he was sorry the King had recovered; better if "he had broken his neck." Rumblings of this kind were rife in the South-East. One Kentish man observed: "It would make the King's heart quake if he knew what his subjects thought about him."

In the north feelings were much like those in the south, but they were potentially more dangerous. The north was more or less an independent state owing more allegiance to its great lords—the Percies and D'Arcies—than to the Tudor King. It is hard to imagine how distant and uninviting the north of England seemed in those days to people living in the south. Henry VIII only paid it one visit—one more than any of his Tudor successors paid. The North was militarily important because of its border with Scotland; but it was cold, wild and desolate country. Northerners had no time for the new-fangled religion creeping up towards them. When it was heard that the monasteries were to be sacked the north rose in revolt in October 1536. This revolt is often known as the Pilgrimage of Grace.

The causes of the revolt were many. Northerners feared the tentacles of central government spreading up from London and a consequent loss of their independence. They resented the great inflation of prices and rents; they resented the fact that in some areas common land was being encroached on by neighbouring farmers for more profitable sheep farming. But basically it was a religious revolt. People just did not like the idea of the King replacing the Pope as head of the Church; they disapproved of the divorce, the ruthless break with Rome, and above all the closing down of the monasteries.

A rising in October 1536 in Lincolnshire was soon quashed by an army under the Duke of Suffolk. But while the rebels were being dispersed news came of a far bigger rising in Yorkshire. Its leader was a Yorkshire lawyer and country gentleman, Robert Aske.

The proposals the rebels put forward to the King were wholly religious. First they wanted Princess Mary legitimized, the Pope's authority to be restored and all

> "Ye shall not enter into this our Pilgrimage of Grace for the Commonwealth, but only for the love that ye do bear unto Almighty God his faith, and to Holy Church militant and the maintenance thereof, to the preservation of the King's person and his issue, to the purifying of the nobility, and to expulse all villein blood and evil counsellors against the Commonwealth from his Grace and his Privy Council of the same." *The "Oath of the Honourable Men" all members of the Pilgrimage of Grace were asked to swear, showing how loyal to the King they were.*

the authority that Henry had taken to be returned to the Church. Henry had simply not the resources to attack them. Without a standing army he was virtually at their mercy.

What saved Henry, and in the end all the religious changes that had come to pass, was the character of their leader, Robert Aske. Aske believed and trusted the King. The Duke of Norfolk went to meet Aske and his rebels and promised that the King would hear their grievances and, if they disbanded and went home, give them a free pardon. Henry did not keep his side of the bargain.

Henry may have had some excuse for this. A minor rising took place on the east coast of Yorkshire, and in February 1537 a ragged army of Cumberland peasants laid siege to Carlisle. This was the opening that Henry wanted. The Duke of Norfolk was sent north to deal with them. The Cumberland uprising was on a much smaller scale than the Pilgrimage of Grace and the traitors were easily crushed. Some seventy peasants were hanged; some on the trees in their own gardens. Aske was now brought to London, tried and sent back to Yorkshire for execution. The Duke of Norfolk rode round the rebellious shires on a bloody assize. He was ruthless and no mercy was given. In all some 216 people were executed.

Henry felt he could breathe again. The great test of his policy was over. He had been near to destruction, but had emerged triumphant. He was powerful and rich. The north would long remember his wrath and fear his royal authority. The monasteries had given him wealth which had won him friends. And above all he had a son and heir.

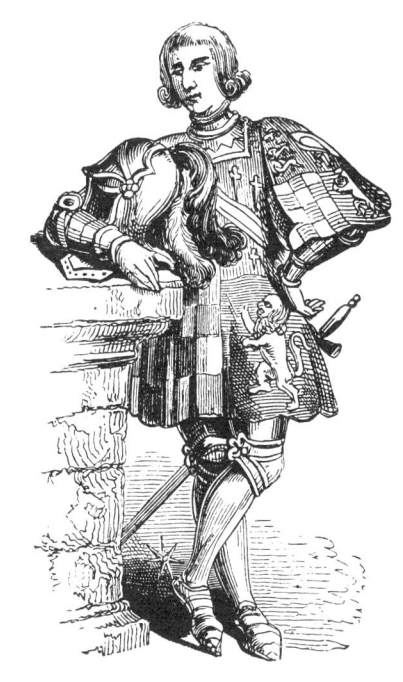

Above John Howard, Duke of Norfolk. At Henry's orders he quelled the uprising in the North of England of 1537.

13 Henry in his Prime

HENRY FELT SECURE. His rebellious subjects were silenced, he had money to spend, and a son to whom he could pass on his throne. He wished now to give his reign a sense of permanence, and to advertise to his subjects his unique power and authority. With all the wealth he had acquired from the monasteries and the plundering of the shrines—no fewer than twenty-six wagons of gold and jewels were pillaged from the shrine of St. Thomas à Becket at Canterbury—he decided to build himself an enormous palace, the like of which would never be seen again.

In a way this was just another example of his intense rivalry and jealousy of Francis I of France. Francis had built a glorious extravaganza of a *chateau* at Chambord. Nonsuch, for that was to be the name of Henry's palace, would comfortably outclass this and become the envy of the civilized world. The Surrey village of Cuddington was destroyed to make way for this spectacular and fantastic monument to Tudor vanity.

Hundreds of craftsmen were imported to work on the project. Materials were taken from the dying abbeys. The building of Nonsuch took three years, completed in 1541. The ornate turrets and pinnacles of the house overlooking 1,200 acres of parkland with 1,000 deer grazing did indeed look fit for a king. The gateway was flanked with statues of the Roman Emperors, but inside in the courtyard stood a massive statue of Henry himself, dwarfing everything, trampling a lion underfoot. There would be no building like it on earth just as there would be no other king like Henry. Yet, like so much of the fruit of Henry's extravagance, it has virtually disappeared from the face of the earth. Today it is

Below Nonsuch Palace, another of Henry's extravagant shows of wealth.

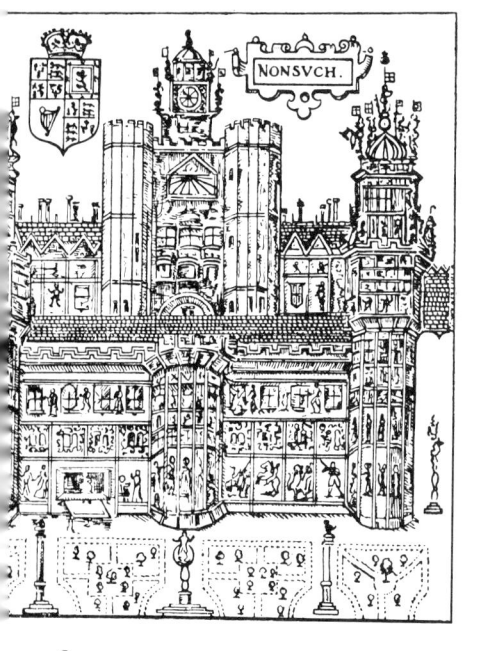

quite hard even to see the foundations.

The King's personal household was remodelled to make it more appropriate for a monarch immortal in the eyes of his subjects. Henry had long envied Francis I's personal bodyguard, and at last in 1539 fifty men were hand-picked for this purpose. These Gentlemen Pensioners had to be at court and attend the King whenever he needed them. But above all they were expert swordsmen and in time of war they could quickly become an elite of highly trained soldiers in Henry's army. In addition to these young men the King's private chamber had sixteen gentlemen, two gentlemen ushers, four usher waiters, three grooms and two barbers. The outer chamber had three cup bearers, three carvers and three sewers. Also, a person was given charge of the King's robes, three officers and two pages for the royal beds. There were, in addition, thirty other grooms and ushers in reserve for the ones attending the King. Far more people now served the King than ever did in the early years of his reign.

The manner of living was regal and the court ate its way through hundreds of tons of food. A typical menu of the period has for its first course, salads of damsons, artichokes, cabbage lettuces, purslane and cucumbers, along with cold dishes of stewed sparrows, carp, capons in lemon, larded pheasants, duck, gulls, forced rabbit, pasty of venison and pear pasty. After these came hot dishes of stork, gannet, heron, pullets, quid, partridge, fresh sturgeon, pasty of venison from red deer, chickens and fritters. As a light refreshment a last course was served of jelly, blancmange, apples, pears with carraway, filberts, syruped cheese with sugar, clotted cream with sugar, quince pie and finally a glass of wine. This was by no means an exceptional menu; the banquets given on state occasions in Whitehall were more extravagant still. Little wonder that the English were acquiring a European reputation for gluttony, and that Henry was getting fat.

Henry had created a quite magnificent court and palace; to ensure its immortality artists, architects and

Below A state banquet of the sixteenth century, typical of the kind of banquet enjoyed by Henry VIII and his court.

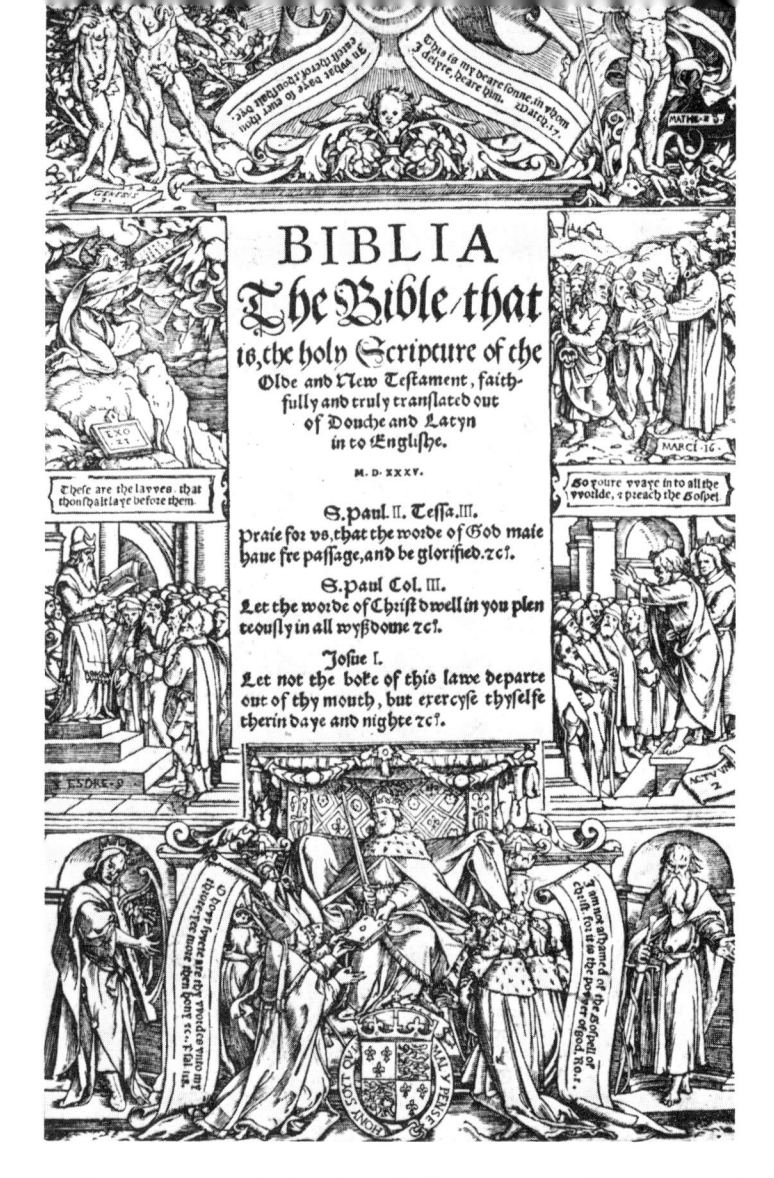

Right The title-page of the first Bible printed in English. The translation was made by Miles Coverdale, and the design was by Hans Holbein.

sculptors were invited to help portray this new-style monarchy. Hans Holbein (1497–1543) is probably the finest artist of Tudor times; his impressions of Henry have given most people their idea of the King's features. In 1536 Thomas Cromwell asked Holbein to design an illustration for the title page of Coverdale's English translation of the Bible. It was to show Henry's idea of monarchy. Holbein pictured Henry enthroned, and whilst holding the sword of justice giving the Bible to his bishops kneeling before him. Opposite, another illustration put Henry firmly in the line of Old Testament prophets and New Testament apostles. This was a vivid and visual interpretation of a King who clearly saw himself as God's representative on earth and answerable only to God.

In addition to its illustrations the Bible had profound theological importance. It had for centuries only been available in Latin translation. To give the Bible to the people in their own native tongue was one of the strongest ideas of the Reformers. There had been earlier English translations but here was an official version, with the King's blessing, to be placed in every parish church in England. This shows clearly how far the Reformers had advanced in the years since the divorce. Besides the legislation of the Reformation Parliament there had been a general drift towards continental Protestantism. Between 1525 and 1547 some eight hundred separate editions of religious works were printed in England, many of them Lutheran. Henry himself never became a Lutheran, but the emergence of Protestantism in the reign of his son Edward VI was made possible by the events in his own.

A group of reformers was pushing Henry further in religious changes than he wished to go. They were led by the Archbishop Thomas Cranmer of Canterbury and Thomas Cromwell. They were in earnest to change the whole style and form of church services. They wished to make the services much simpler, with the priest doing without elaborate vestments, and the hymns and prayers all in English. They wanted to take out of the churches everything that seemed idolatrous, for example statues of the Virgin Mary; and to make the priests themselves seem much more homely men by letting them marry. By careful planning Cromwell had been able to introduce one or two of these ideas with the King's approval. He had ordered the dismantling of the holy shrines and places of pilgrimage and of course had ordered an English Bible to be placed in every village church.

> "When the King had allowed the Bible to be set forth to be read in all the churches, immediately several poor men in the town of Chelmsford in Essex bought the New Testament and on Sundays sat reading of it in the lower end of the church: many would flock about them to hear their reading." *Showing the effect of Henry's Bible from "The Narrative of William Maldon of Newington."*

Cromwell's secular policy had been no less striking than his religious one. Basically he streamlined the mediaeval system of government into something more suitable for a modern European state. The old system, which Wolsey had not touched, was based firmly and squarely on the King. Now Cromwell devised a system in which the King's business was split up into various departments, run by efficient experts with secretaries and clerks to help them. Thus in a crude form we can see the modern method of government taking shape, in which a cabinet minister is responsible for a department such as health or education, helped by a skilled team of professional civil servants. By the early 1540s, Cromwell's system had replaced the old one in which the King was personally in charge of everything.

All orders were written down on paper. Gone were the days when business was transacted by word of mouth only. Henry's father, Henry VII, had personally supervised the accounts of the Exchequer and himself kept an up-to-date record of the nation's finances. This became unthinkable in the last few years of Henry VIII's reign. People began to talk of national revenue and not the King's finances.

A tighter and more professional system in London led the country as a whole to feel the effect of Cromwell's "good governance." A much tighter grip could be kept on the powerful barons out of London and likely rebels. There was only one serious rebellion in Henry's reign, due largely to Cromwell's reorganization of the old councils that had dominated the north, and Wales. By bringing these outlying areas of the kingdom under central control the feeling of unity—of belonging to one nation—became more evident.

More and more power was being given to people other than the King and Cromwell was directing affairs much to his own liking; but ultimately Henry was always firmly in control. He let Cromwell go his own way only because his reforms and ideas of government fitted his idea of kingship perfectly. They made his power more absolute.

Below Henry VIII delivering the new Bible to Archbishop Cranmer and Thomas Cromwell to circulate around the land.

14 Henry and his New Queen

IN THE DIFFICULT YEARS following his divorce from Catherine of Aragon, and the resulting break with Rome, Henry had been able to pursue his own affairs, free to forget Europe. Europe, in turn, had been quite content to forget Henry; once again it was embroiled in a struggle between Francis I and Emperor Charles V. However, on 18th June 1538 Charles and Francis agreed to a ten year truce. This was a danger signal to Henry. Now they could turn to rooting out Protestant heretics and restoring the old Catholic religion. Furthermore the Pope issued a decree declaring Henry no longer King of England and called upon Catholics everywhere to attack him. It looked as if the long threatened "Catholic crusade" was about to begin.

England became convulsed with war panic. She was without a friend in Europe and could become, as Thomas Wriothesley, one of Cromwell's henchmen and a leading Privy Councillor, said, "but a vessel amongst these choppers." Peasants and townsfolk were drilled and mustered, ditches were dug, barricades and warning beacons were prepared in the event of an invasion across the Channel.

Cromwell obviously thought the situation dangerous enough to suggest that Henry looked for a fourth wife. After all, Jane Seymour was dead through childbirth, and a foreign wife could be very useful. To find a politically suitable bride turned out to be harder than expected. There were quite a few desirable young ladies in Europe. There was Francis I's daughter Margaret, and Marie, daughter of the Duke of Guise and Christina, widow of the Duke of Milan. All these came to nothing. When one remembers England's religious upheavals

Below A castle on the South Downs, equipped and ready to repel an invasion. When the Pope called on Catholics everywhere to rise up against England, Henry became obsessed with the idea of being invaded, and prepared his people to meet the challenge.

> "If it were not to satisfy the world and my realm I would not do that I must do this day for none earthly thing." *Henry VIII talking to Cromwell just before his marriage with Anne of Cleves.*

> "I see nothing in this woman as men report of her and I marvel that wise men should make such reports as they have done. ... If I had known as much before as I know now, she should never have come into this realm." *Henry VIII talking to his advisers the night after he had seen Anne of Cleves for the first time.*

and Henry's marital record, it is not surprising that none of these ladies were anxious to be the next Queen of England.

But Henry was keen. He had worked his overweight frame into quite a frenzy of amour. There were other ladies to be considered besides these and not knowing whom to choose he asked Francis to let the eligible ladies meet him at Calais. There he would inspect them all, as if judging some beauty contest, and choose his bride. Francis, about to make his peace with Charles, was not interested; Henry would have to look elsewhere.

Attention was centred on Cleves. This was a small German principality straddling the southern reaches of the River Rhine. Lutheranism had been gaining ground in Germany and had become the official religion of several German states. The Duke of Cleves was a Protestant, and one of several Lutheran princes who had banded together against Charles who was determined to keep his Empire Catholic. An alliance between Cleves and England would not give Charles too many sleepless nights, but it might make him a little uncomfortable.

Thomas Cromwell was enthusiastic about the proposed alliance. When he learned that the Duke had two daughters, Amelia and Anne, Henry became quite ecstatic. In August 1539, Hans Holbein was sent off to paint their portraits. When the artist returned, the royal choice was Anne, and while she made her way to England preparations were put in hand for her reception and eventual marriage.

The prospect of love and romance had made the middle-aged Henry gay and lighthearted again. Forgetting his ever-present aches and pains he could not wait to see Anne in the flesh, so appealing did she look in Holbein's portrait.

At last the moment arrived. Henry should have waited to greet her in London, but he was too impatient for that. When he heard in December 1539 that she had arrived in England he dressed up with five of his courtiers in marbled cloaks and hoods, and made his way to the port of Rochester to meet her. Here he entered her chamber disguised as one of his own messengers. Anne was taken aback, especially when the King tried to embrace her. When Henry revealed his true identity she could only stare blankly through a window into the courtyard. There was no conversation between the couple as Anne could not speak English. Henry was bitterly disappointed. Now it was his anger, not his passion, that was aroused.

Henry felt he had been cheated and betrayed. The original portrait by Holbein has been lost but the copy in the Louvre Museum in Paris suggests a plain country girl. Cromwell had pushed for the marriage on political grounds and had probably suppressed some reports about Anne's plainness; but Henry himself was most to blame for Anne's coolness, with his vain and bombastic manner. After all, Anne was a timid girl in a strange country, with no English, completely unused to the King's overpowering ways. Henry felt at once that she was frigid, a complete let down to all his expectations. He never once tried to make the relationship work.

He was so incensed that he tried to wriggle out of the marriage altogether. The wedding was put off for two days, but no diplomatic way was found of cancelling it. The wedding took place on 6th January 1540, but the marriage was never consummated. Anne could never bring herself to face this huge and grotesque figure of a man, while Henry could raise no spark of enthusiasm either for Anne's character or her physical features. A divorce was on the cards even before the wedding ceremony, and when it came in July 1540, after just six months of loveless marriage, Anne was quite relieved to retire peacefully to the English countryside with two houses and a pension of £500 a year.

The full force of Henry's anger at being tricked, as he felt, into marriage with Anne of Cleves was directed against the man who had arranged it all, Thomas Cromwell. In the face of his master's wrath Cromwell's fall was swift, certain, and final. On 18th April 1540, he had been made Earl of Essex and sometime before this Lord Great Chamberlain of the royal household. Yet on

Above Anne of Cleves, the fourth wife of Henry VIII. A portrait by Hans Holbein.

10th June 1540 he was arrested by a captain of the guard. At first he refused to believe the order and threw down his hat in anger, but soon the awful reality of the situation dawned on him and he was led to the Tower.

Why did Henry so ruthlessly cut down perhaps the ablest of all his servants? He was in a very disturbed mental state. He had worked himself up into a frenzy of excitement over Anne of Cleves; he was bitterly disappointed. Now, with almost indecent haste, Henry began to show an interest in a girl of nineteen, Catherine Howard (1521–42), a niece of the Duke of Norfolk. His temperature rose again at the prospect. His mind was such that he would listen to any advice, no matter how illogical, if it came from someone close to young Catherine. The Duke of Norfolk was a Catholic; Cromwell was a Protestant. The Duke hated the way Cromwell had led Henry into destroying the Church he knew and loved.

Henry's own religious views are hard to make out. The evidence we do have only supports the view that the King was egotistic. He seemed only interested in dogma which touched his own position and authority. He had no interest in promoting individual liberty. Whatever reforms were carried out seemed only to enhance the King's own power. To be Supreme Head of the Church gave him God's authority on earth, which could never be questioned, even by his bishops. Once he had what he wanted Henry was quite conservative at heart. The masses in the royal chapel, the priests clothed in vestments, the glorious music—it all looked much the same as in the old days.

Henry's conservative outlook was reinforced after the Pilgrimage of Grace. The civil dangers of pushing ahead too far and too fast with reforming the Church were obvious. Henry became alarmed and thought it was time to call a halt. With the publication of the six Acts in 1539 many people thought that Henry had turned the clock back. These Acts upheld traditional Catholic beliefs such as celibacy of the clergy, confession and communion only in one kind for the laity. Henry certainly did not want to undo anything that he had done so far—but he wished to go no further. Falling more and more under Norfolk's Catholic influence, Henry had grown suspicious of Cromwell's motives.

A proud aristocrat, the Duke of Norfolk hated the upstart Cromwell as much for his lowly birth as for his Protestantism. In this he was joined by most aristocratic members of Henry's court. Here was their chance for revenge. At first they tried to prove that in 1538 Cromwell had said he would marry Princess Mary and make himself king. This seemed, even to Norfolk, too crazy to be taken seriously. They settled in the end on a charge of treason, saying that Cromwell had helped to spread subversive Lutheran literature and generally helped the Lutheran cause in England. Cromwell's trial was a cruel sham. He was tried by Act of Attainder, which denied him a fair hearing. Inevitably he was found guilty of high treason, and on 18th July 1540 he was executed on Tower Hill.

Henry had struck down first Wolsey, now Cromwell. Never again would he rely on any political figure. Even in Cromwell's time Henry had spent far more time on affairs of state than he had earlier in his reign. In future, he decided there could be only one chief minister—himself.

> "For as I ever have had love to your honour, person, life, prosperity, health, wealth, joy and comfort.... God so help me in this mine adversity and confound me if ever I thought the contrary! For if it were in my power to make your Majesty to live ever young and prosperous, God knoweth I would. If it had been in my power to make you rich ... I would do it ... for your Majesty hath been the most bountiful prince to me that ever was King to his subject." *Cromwell writing to Henry from the Tower of London (June 1540).*

15 Henry's Last Wives

Below Catherine Howard, fifth wife of Henry VIII.

HENRY VIII shed no crocodile tears for Cromwell. It would have been out of character if he had. In any case he was far too busy with young Catherine Howard. Catherine had come to court at the end of 1539 when she was appointed a maid of honour to Anne of Cleves. The moment he set eyes on her Henry became infatuated. His passions were aroused and as soon as he was legally divorced from Anne he married his young and delectable bride. The wedding took place on the same day that Cromwell was executed—18th July 1540.

Henry was a paunchy pain-racked figure of 49. His young bride was only 20. Catherine was by common consent by far the most attractive of his six wives. To Henry, fast becoming an old man, the prospect of love and friendship with a woman in the bloom of youth made a new man of him. Catherine, for her part, accepted Henry. As Queen she would obviously become a very powerful and influential person in the realm. Henry was in high good humour and showered gifts upon her. At the Christmas festivities of 1540 he gave her a "square containing 27 table diamonds and 26 clusters of pearls." In addition he gave her the lands and estates of Jane Seymour and Thomas Cromwell. The court of Henry VIII enjoyed an Indian summer of revelry, jousting and feasting as extravagant and colourful as any in the earlier years of the reign.

But it was not to last. Within eighteen months of the marriage Catherine would be dead. Girls in the early sixteenth century had a strict upbringing; they were chaperoned and protected from contact with men until they were safely married off. Although Catherine was the niece of a great Duke she had an ill-disciplined and lax upbringing. Her mother died before she was ten and her father could not be bothered with her and left her under the control of her step-grandmother, the Dowager Duchess of Norfolk. The Dowager seems to have let Catherine do as she pleased and before long she was making love with her music teacher behind the altar in the family chapel. These sex games went on and chief of her admirers was her cousin, Francis Dereham.

When Catherine became Queen she invited Dereham to court as her private secretary. Her affair with Dereham was still going on. Two other courtiers, members of the Privy Chamber, caught her eye too, Thomas Paston and Thomas Culpeper. Perhaps we cannot blame her for wanting the company of younger men. Henry by this time must have presented a terrifying spectacle to any young woman. Gone for ever were the signs of athletic grace. Henry now presented a grim picture of sagging jaws and swollen features. His eyelids were always half closed as if in continual pain. The ulcer on his leg had grown far worse. There was a time shortly before his marriage when his ulcer had clogged and caused a terrible blockage in his lungs. This had made him black in the face and speechless. With the exertion and excitement of his marriage this ulcer closed up completely, preventing any pus from escaping. The resultant pain was agonizing and brought on a period of black despondency.

Confronted with a husband more than twice her age, of moody temper, with a running sore on his leg, and his whole body obese and grotesque, no wonder a young vivacious girl of twenty would choose companions of her own age. But to do so was to court disaster. Catherine threw caution to the winds. When Henry made his grand tour of the north in the summer of 1541, Catherine and her lady-in-waiting, Lady Rochford, conspired to smuggle Thomas Culpeper into her bedchamber. It was only a game, but a highly dangerous one. Sooner or later the King was bound to find out.

When the King first heard of Catherine's indiscretion he simply would not believe it of her. However, he did

> "The King is so amorous of Catherine Howard that he cannot treat her well enough and caresses her more than he did the others." *Charles de Marillac, French Ambassador in London writing to a friend (September 1540).*

> "The King . . . being solicited by his Council to marry again took to wife Catherine, daughter of the late Edmund Howard, thinking now in his old age to have obtained a jewel for womanhood, but this joy is turned to extreme sorrow . . . having heard that she was not a woman of such purity as was esteemed." *The Privy Council to Sir William Reget, Henry's ambassador to France (November 1541).*

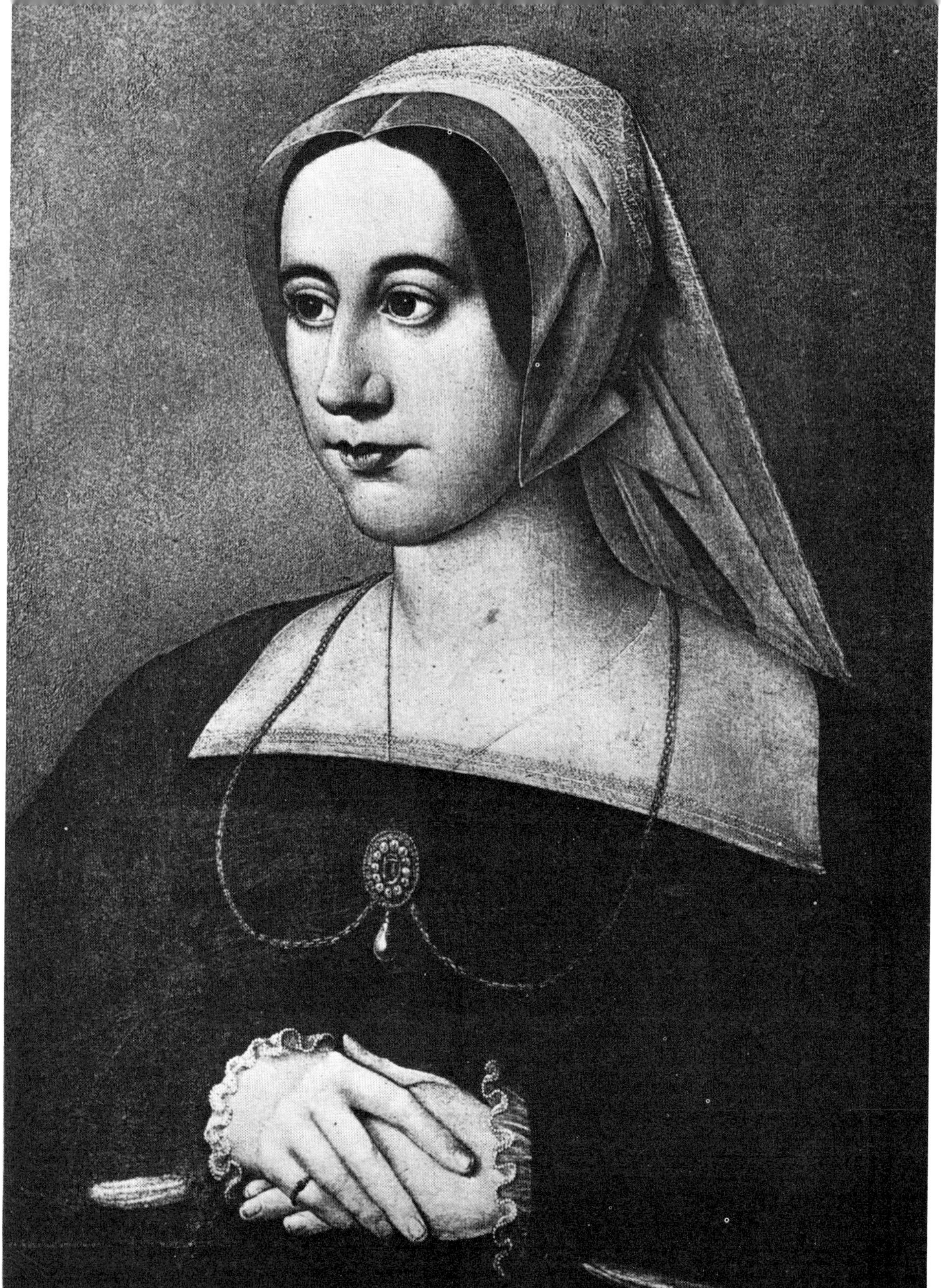

set up an investigating committee. When the evidence of Catherine's adultery was laid plainly before him his former tenderness and passion for the girl exploded into uncontrollable wrath. The King had been humiliated. God's self-appointed representative on earth had been tricked by a cheap little bitch. In his unstoppable rage the Queen, Dereham, Culpeper, Mannox, her music teacher, and Lady Rochford were all executed in February 1542. Divorce for an adulterous Queen was too lenient. The husband who was head of Church and state demanded the severest penalty.

After his bitter disappointment with the young Catherine, it is surprising that Henry would wish to marry again. Yet now, almost completely immobile and suffering ever-worsening pain from his leg, he needed the solace and comfort of a woman. Eighteen months after Catherine's execution, in July 1543, he married Catherine Parr (1512–48). This was to prove a far better choice. Catherine was in her early thirties and had already been married twice. One day, after seeing Henry buried, she would marry a fourth husband.

She was to prove a mature and patient companion for his last difficult years. In the spring of 1544 Henry's ulcerous leg flared up again. Defying palace convention Catherine moved her bed into a small chamber near the King's bedroom so she could comfort him in his illness. The accounts we have of Catherine's apothecary show the real care and concern she felt for her husband. There were preservative lozenges, cinnamon comfits, liquorice pastilles, plasters for the spleen and sponges for fomentations for dressing his leg. She probably made Henry get some reading glasses to ease the strain on his eyes.

Besides acting as his nurse she tried to be a mother to his children. Mary, Elizabeth and Edward had not enjoyed a secure family life. The two princesses had lived most of their lives in fear and contempt of their father. Now for the first time Catherine attempted to weld them into a family unit. She engaged tutors for them and held daily classes for their instruction. Thanks to Catherine, Henry's last years were made as comfortable as possible.

Left Catherine Parr, sixth wife of Henry VIII.

16 War and Death

IT WAS A MOST DIFFICULT task to control and calm Henry. In that decaying carcass there still burned undimmed a desire for adventure and youth. He could never come to terms with his loss of physical powers. As a sort of release, and a last chance to relive the glories of youth, he turned his mind to war.

In the summer of 1542 the age-old dispute between Emperor Charles V and Francis I of France had flared up once again. Francis was seeking revenge for his defeat at Pavia in 1525. Both he and Charles wished to be supreme in Europe, and there were bound to be wars in their rivalry. Now seemed the ideal opportunity for Henry to achieve his dream to reconquer the mediaeval English empire in France.

Before any major effort against France could be undertaken the border with Scotland must first be secured. Throughout the summer of 1542 English troops developed their strength along the border. The Scottish King James V (1512–42) was asked in September to sign a treaty that would in effect make Scotland a satellite state of England. Naturally he refused. The Duke of Norfolk was despatched to the north to teach the Scots a lesson. The Duke who had burdened the King with two adulterous nieces, Anne and Catherine, was anxious to please him. He led an army on a six-day raid around the Scottish town of Kelso, pillaging and looting. In retaliation the Scottish army counter-attacked and marched south toward Carlisle. Though superior in strength, the Scots army literally got bogged down in Solway Moss on 23rd November 1542. Few soldiers were killed but many were taken prisoner, including most of the Scottish nobility. When he heard the news James V was heart-

Below James V of Scotland. Father of Mary Queen of Scots, his army was taken prisoner at Solway Moss in 1542. Heartbroken, he died a few days after the defeat.

broken and within a few days was dead from shock and disgrace. His only heir was his week-old daughter, Mary Queen of Scots (1542–87).

Scotland lay at Henry's feet. But to Henry a backward and barbaric kingdom with a mere babe on the throne was of no interest. France was the real prize and it was south, not north, that the King turned his attention. This was the project that obliterated all others in his mind. At the end of December 1543 a treaty between Henry and Charles was signed in London whereby each monarch promised to invade France in the following summer. Henry became wildly excited about the forthcoming expedition and was absolutely determined to be there in person to supervise and observe events.

Early in June 1544 a vast English force sailed over to Calais led by the veteran war lords, the Dukes of Norfolk and Suffolk. By mid June they had begun to march eastwards into France. Henry disembarked in Calais on 14th July 1544, borne on a litter. There seemed to be a general air of uncertainty and disorganization. There was also a general shortage of bread, beer, guns and shot. Soon after Henry arrived, the Duke of Suffolk went to look at the lie of the land around Boulogne. On the 19th July the English army besieged the town. Bad weather held things up and not until early August did the full battery of English guns open up against the walls. Henry had a fine time. He supervised every move and seemed to be in better spirits and health than he had for years. On the 11th September Boulogne castle was blown up and on the 14th the English delivered their terms for the town's capitulation. These were reluctantly accepted and on the 18th Henry entered Boulogne in triumph. He stayed twelve days supervising its fortification by his troops and after knighting some of his soldiers returned home on 30th September.

The capture of Boulogne proved to be the one high spot of the expedition. On the same day as Henry entered Boulogne, Francis and Charles made their peace. This left Henry in the lurch and his army in a dangerous situation. Henry ordered the Duke of Nor-

Above Mary Queen of Scots. Her father, James V, having been defeated by Henry VIII, she ironically became a thorn in the flesh of Henry's daughter, Elizabeth I. Her own fate was no kinder, however; Elizabeth had her executed at the block.

Above The English forces drawn up at Portsmouth in July, 1544, before the expedition into France to attack the French army under Francis I.

"We are at war with France and Scotland, we have enmity with the Bishop of Rome, we have no assured friendship here with the Emperor and we have received from the landgrave, chief captain of the Protestants, such displeasure that he has cause to think us angry with him. Our war is noisome to our realm and to all our merchants that traffic through the Narrow Seas. We are in a world where reason and learning prevail not and covenants are little regarded." *Stephen Gardiner, Bishop of Winchester, writing in pessimistic mood about England's position in 1545.*

folk, who was marching further into French territory, to pull back to Boulogne. Three days after Henry came back to England he heard the alarming news that the Dukes of Norfolk and Suffolk had led the army out of Boulogne and retreated to Calais. Henry was furious. He ordered the army back to their posts in Boulogne, but this was quite out of the question. The English army was trapped in Calais and surrounded by an enemy force of 50,000 men. There was nothing to do but get into the ships and sail home. In truth, it was an apt end to a campaign which had always been disorganized and was now ending in a complete muddle.

England was isolated without a real friend in Europe and once again the country was gripped by an invasion scare. In the summer of 1545 three armies of 30,000 men were drawn up in Essex, Kent and the West. On the 10th August 1545 hymns and prayers were offered up in every parish church to ask God for victory.

In the middle of June Francis I had been to Rouen to inspect his fleet of over 200 ships before it sailed for England. On 19th July this fleet entered the Solent at the very moment Henry VIII was dining aboard the *Great Harry*. As soon as the French armada was sighted the King hastily went ashore and ordered a series of beacons to be lit across England, warning the people of an imminent invasion. Several small skirmishes took place between the rival fleets, but in the end the Channel weather won the victory. First the English fleet was becalmed and then a north-east gale prevented any more action and the French sailed home.

This was probably not a serious invasion attempt; rather it was a clear hint from Francis that the English had better evacuate Boulogne quickly before worse things happened. However, the episode did serve to underline England's unique defensive strength as an island, and its need for a strong navy to ward off any likely invader. Henry has often been called the "father of the English Navy" and the title is fully justified.

Henry had inherited seven battle ships from his father. By 1514 he had twenty-four more and by the end of the reign he had built up a sizeable fighting force. In addition to increasing the numbers the very style of the ships was altered. The old mediaeval fighting ship was a sort of floating platform. The guns were only effective at close quarters. The main purpose of the ship was to sail close to the enemy's vessel and allow the soldiers on board to fight hand to hand. Sea warfare was only an extension of fighting on land.

The new-style Tudor ship was essentially a floating battery. It was a long slim vessel, with a low port and forecastle, and one, two or even more rows of gun ports. The guns themselves became bigger and more effective. Sea-warfare took on a new style. Hand-to-hand fighting gave way to the broadside, the familiar form of sea battle right up to modern times.

The transformation of the English navy was far from complete at the end of Henry's reign, but it had begun. Old ships such as the *Great Harry* were refitted with extra gun ports in their waists. The dry-dock at Portsmouth was enlarged and Woolwich dockyard was built in 1514. At the end of Henry's reign a new Navy Board was set up to look after naval affairs. The modern English navy was taking shape.

How far these improvements were due to Henry's

Above The *Harry Grace-à-Dieu*, or *Great Harry*, the ship built for Henry in 1512.

personal initiative it is hard to say; but his great love of ships and interest in them would certainly have encouraged and promoted reform. He had been closely involved in putting together the royal fleet for his first French expedition in 1513. He loved to visit his ships and watch them on exercises and manoeuvres. Once when he was visiting Southampton he had the guns of his galleys "fired again and again making their range, as he is very curious about matters of this kind."

> "Now, since I find such kindness on your part toward me, I cannot choose but love and favour you, affirming that no prince in the world more favoureth his subjects than I do you, Nor no subjects or commons more love and obey their sovereign lord than I perceive you do me." *The opening of Henry VIII's last speech to Parliament showing his concern for his subjects. It partly explains the veneration in which Henry was held by most Englishmen.*

The disappearance of the French fleet did not mean the end of Henry's problems. Once again he was desperately short of money. The war with Scotland and France had cost some £2,200,000. Monastic lands that had been put on one side by Thomas Cromwell were now hurriedly sold off to bring in some ready cash. Some £800,000 came from this source. In addition, his subjects had to pay out heavier taxes than ever before. Yet Henry was still short of cash, and so began the debasement of the coinage. The whole exercize, like other expedients, was done for a quick cash return regardless of serious long term consequences to the nation. Although they still had the same face value, Henry's new coins contained less real silver and gold. The surplus gold and silver of course went to help Henry out of his financial difficulty. This measure alone yielded more than a quarter of a million pounds. Depressingly, even this was not enough and Henry was forced to go cap in hand to the financial houses of Antwerp and borrow money at 10% and 14% interest. These loans mounted and at his death totalled some £75,000.

These desperate measures, certainly that of the debasement of the currency, simply stored up more trouble for the future, notably in the form of inflation. In the last years of Henry's reign prices mounted steadily. The thriving businessman of the cities could cope with this, but, as always, the poorer classes suffered. The peasant farmer found it ever harder to manage with the rising prices, and Henry himself only succeeded in buying time. Grave social unrest was bound to follow the inflation, though it was to be his son Edward VI and

Left Henry VIII, after Hans Holbein.

his ministers that were to pay the price for Henry's short-sighted measures.

The reign that had opened in summer brilliance and had promised so much was drawing to a close in dark and chilly days. The King now was almost completely immobile. He was carried everywhere by litter. His leg was worse and he was subject to frequent fevers. It was obvious that Henry was dying.

With the King now visibly sinking towards death the court became a place of intrigue and of jockeying for positions in the next reign. Rival groups of Protestant and Roman Catholic sympathies were formed hoping to get the upper hand over the youthful Prince Edward. No-one could find the courage to tell Henry how near he was to death. To tell a monarch this would have been an act of treason. Such was the respect and fear that his court still felt for Henry that not until 27th January 1547 did Sir Anthony Denny, the chief gentleman of the Chamber, advise the King "to prepare himself to death."

After a few hours' sleep Henry asked to see his old friend Thomas Cranmer. The King was now nearly

> "And for my body, which when the soul is departed, shall then remain but as a 'cadaver', and so return to the vile matter it was made of, were it not for the crown and dignity which God hath called us unto, and that We would not be counted an infringer of honest worldly policies and customs, when they be not contrary to God's laws, We would be content to have it buried in any place accustomed to Christian folks. . . . Nevertheless because We would be loth . . . to do injury to the Dignity, which we are unworthyly called unto, We are content to will and order that Our body be buried and intered in the choir of Our college at Windsor." *Henry VIII justifying in his will at some length the reason for his wish to be buried at Windsor.*

speechless and unconscious. He clasped Cranmer's hand firmly. Cranmer was the sole survivor of the days when England had stood alone against Pope and Emperor, and Henry clearly regarded him as a close friend. When the Archbishop asked for some token that his master put his trust in Christ, Henry "holding him with his hand, dug using his hand in his as hard as he could." At two o'clock on the morning of Friday, 28th January 1547, King Henry VIII of England died.

For three days the news of his death was kept a secret, but then the Houses of Parliament were told of Henry's death. News travels quickly and on 8th February a solemn dirge was sung in every parish church in England for the old King's memory. The following day a requiem mass was offered for the King's soul. One week later he was buried beside Jane Seymour in the chapel at Windsor. In his will he asked that daily masses "while the world shall endure" should be said for his soul. These masses are no longer said. Even his widow Catherine Parr was soon to marry her fourth husband, Thomas Seymour.

17 Henry, King and Emperor

HENRY WAS DEAD, but his memory lives on. Perhaps after his daughter Queen Elizabeth I and Queen Victoria, Henry is the most remembered of all England's monarchs. He has through the centuries become a part of English folklore, almost a legendary figure. Yet does he deserve our attention as a statesman, and has he the right to be considered a great king?

Henry was in his 57th year when he died, and he had reigned for 37 years and 8 months. To have survived so long and died in his own bed is in itself a remarkable achievement for those violent post-mediaeval times. He had survived attempts on his throne, shrugged off excommunication by the Pope and lived through an invasion scare to deliver to his young son a peaceful kingdom and secure throne. Although only nine years old Edward came to the throne unchallenged, clear proof of the success of the first two Tudors to see that their line was established and respected in England.

Whether Henry died a Catholic or not it is hard to say. The Six Acts, as we have seen, significantly halted the King's apparent conversion to Lutheranism. But it did not mean that Catholicism was restored; the old order went on being gradually eroded. Cromwell may have been destroyed by Norfolk's Catholic party but Archbishop Cranmer stayed on. Henry never abandoned him. In February 1543 Henry gave his assent to a project of Cranmer's to amend the Breviary. This bore fruit in the next reign in the prayer book which gave the Church of England forms of service largely unaltered to this day. Henry even thought of turning the Mass into a communion service and more significantly saw that his son had religious reformers to tutor him. As Prince

Below The medal struck to commemorate the coronation of Edward VI.

Above Stephen Gardiner, Bishop of Winchester.

"He ruled in a ruthless age with a ruthless hand, he dealt with a violent crisis by methods of blood and iron, and his measures were crowned with whatever sanction worldly success can give.... The spiritual welfare of England entered into his thoughts, if at all, as a minor consideration; but for her peace and material comfort it was well that she had as her King, in her hour of need, a man, and a man who counted the cost, who faced the risk, and who did with his might whatsoever his hand found to do." *Henry VIII, Arthur Pollard (1902).*

Edward would be so young when he came to the throne, a council of leading ministers would act on his behalf until he was old enough to do the job. Again it is interesting to see that most of the council nominated by Henry were Protestant; Stephen Gardiner (1485–1555), Bishop of Winchester and leading member of the Catholic Party, was left out.

In the end perhaps Henry's most enduring achievement was to bring into being a national Church. In the process he had defied both Pope and Emperor and appointed himself the Church's supreme head, endowing English kingship with a new dimension and a new dignity. By his acts the whole style and character of much of English country life had changed when the monasteries were pulled down. Unwittingly maybe, Henry led his people towards a complete break with the old religion by sanctioning the English Bible, which opened the way to an English prayer book with all services spoken in the native tongue.

Politically Henry's reign endowed England with a new sense of national identity. With the end of an independent Church, the absorption of the kingdom of Wales and the setting up of two strong councils in the North and West, England was more unified than ever before. The machinery of government under Thomas Cromwell was much more efficient and far-reaching. Under his regime society shed some of its violent and rebellious characteristics, and the "over-mighty" subject was less able or inclined to go his own way. Never before had England felt the power of the state so widely and deeply as in the 1530s and 1540s. Everyone in the land, whether by swearing the Oath of Succession or of Supremacy or experiencing some of the sweeping changes made by Parliament, would one day in their lives feel this power; because of it they would feel a sense of nationality as never before.

Henry VIII was a huge majestical figure. To most of his subjects he was a natural-born king—a bluff, corpulent, England-loving leader. Through all the ups and downs of his reign his people had followed him, sometimes eagerly, sometimes grudgingly. But they had followed and by the end of his reign he was a respected, even a loved figure.

Yet for all his show of warmth and genial swagger he rarely performed a true act of kindness. The two people he loved most—Jane Seymour and Thomas Cranmer—would certainly have been executed if they had stood in his way. The King was always in control. He would not tolerate any contradiction. His vanity and arrogance demanded that he should always be at the centre of events, and that everything should be dependent on his will.

Henry was always looking for platforms to show the world his greatness. To this end he led England three times into a war with France. The only result was a colossal loss of resources and waste of money. Where he could have led his armies with some effect —Scotland—he left in a state of bloody confusion. For all his good work with the navy he did not encourage his sailors to explore new worlds. There was one half-hearted attempt, but by and large the challenge of America was ignored and all attention was focussed on the old world of Europe.

Henry had inherited a vast fortune from his careful father. Within a few years this had been squandered in wars and high living. After the dissolution of the monasteries he again became a rich man. With this wealth he could have established a system of education or provided hospitals for the poor. We have seen earlier his love of learning, and the intellectual climate would have been fairly ripe to open many schools and colleges. A number of schools were founded, notably at Canterbury, Ely and Worcester, but in the main the opportunity was lost. The money of the monasteries was spilled on the battlefields of Europe in Henry's vain quest for glory. If Henry had lived cautiously this money could have placed the English monarchy in a financially impregnable position. Fortunately for the future of English society as a whole he died in debt, dependent upon Parliamentary grants.

"Maybe Henry was no more unaware and irresponsible than many Kings have been: but rarely, if ever, have the unawareness and irresponsibility of a King proved more costly of material benefit to his people." *Henry VIII, J.J. Scarisbrick (1968).*

There can be no question that Henry was vain, self-seeking and ambitious. To satisfy a whim or settle a personal score he would unfeelingly destroy a man or a whole town. His reign witnessed more destruction of beautiful buildings, stained glass and ornament than since the coming of the Vikings. Yet for all his faults Henry deserves our admiration. Through the respect for his authority he engendered in his subjects, England was spared the excesses of European violence. Without his strong and effective leadership, in the mould of the first Henry Tudor, England might well have slipped back into a state of civil anarchy. Throughout the turmoil that went with the changeover from the Church of Rome to the Church of England, and the strengthening of central government, Henry was always firmly in control. Thanks to a powerful and at times ruthless style of kingship Henry bequeathed a realm which, eventually, under his daughter Queen Elizabeth, was able to withstand the might of Spain and to become one of the major powers of Europe.

> "Henry's reign in many ways left a deeper mark on the rural heart and face of England than did any event in English history between the coming of the Normans and the coming of the factory." *Henry VIII, J. J. Scarisbrick (1968).*

The Six Wives of Henry VIII

CATHERINE OF ARAGON (1485–1536), first wife of Henry VIII, the youngest daughter of Ferdinand and Isabella of Spain. Married Arthur in 1501. Married Henry in 1509. Between 1510 and 1518 bore five children, only Mary surviving. Divorced from Henry in 1533. After divorce lived at Ampthill and Kimbolton Castle, Hunts., where she died in 1536, probably of cancer of the heart.

ANNE BOLEYN (1504–1536), second wife of Henry VIII, niece of the Duke of Norfolk. Her sister was one of Henry's mistresses. Anne's relationship with Henry began in earnest in 1527 following the opening of divorce proceedings with Catherine of Aragon. Married to Henry in January 1533. Gave birth to Elizabeth in September 1533. In May 1536 she was executed on charges of adultery.

JANE SEYMOUR (1509–1537), third wife of Henry VIII, the daughter of Sir John Seymour. Married Henry in 1536. Gave birth to Edward and died shortly afterwards in 1537.

ANNE OF CLEVES (1515–1557), fourth wife of Henry VIII, the daughter of the Duke of Cleves. Married Henry in 1540 and was divorced six months later after a loveless marriage.

CATHERINE HOWARD (1521–1542), the fifth wife of Henry VIII. Married Henry in the same month that he was divorced from Anne of Cleves, July 1540. Charged in November 1541 with committing adultery with various persons. Executed in February 1542.

CATHERINE PARR (1512–1548), the sixth wife of Henry VIII. She married Henry, her third husband, in July 1543. Managed to reconcile Henry to his daughters Mary and Elizabeth. Very soon after Henry's death (1547) she married a former lover, Sir Thomas Seymour. Died in 1548 in childbirth.

Principal Characters

CLEMENT VII (1523–34). Pope at the time of the divorce proceedings between Henry and Catherine of Aragon. Somewhat lacking in judgement, he allied himself with Francis I, which led to the sacking of Rome by Charles V. As a result he was a prisoner of Charles and mainly because of this he refused to allow Henry his divorce which led to the severing of all ties between England and Rome.

CHARLES V (1500–58). Elected Holy Roman Emperor in 1519. For much of his life concerned with wars with France. Also tried to rid his Empire of Protestantism. More often than not Henry VIII was Charles' ally, but Charles always held the upper hand and often dictated terms.

CRANMER, THOMAS (1489–1556). Educated at Cambridge University and for much of his early life a tutor there. In 1529 he came into prominence by suggesting that an appeal to the universities of Europe be made over the divorce question. In 1532 he was made Archbishop of Canterbury. He helped Henry to divorce Queen Catherine and made the marriage to Anne Boleyn legal. Henry never allowed his priests to marry but Cranmer had for all the time he was Archbishop a "secret" wife. He is chiefly remembered for the Prayer Book which he published in Edward's reign. His refusal to recant his Protestantism led to his death in 1556 in the reign of Queen Mary.

CROMWELL, THOMAS (1485–1540). Son of a Putney blacksmith, brewer and innkeeper. In his early manhood a mercenary soldier on the continent. On his return to England (1513) he quickly made his name as a merchant and lawyer. In 1523 he entered Parliament. He became Wolsey's secretary in 1525. After Wolsey's fall he became Henry VIII's right hand man. Engineered much of the work of the Reformation Parliament. (The Act of Supremacy (1534) and the Dissolution of the Monasteries (1536–39).) Among his many posts were Privy Councillor (1531), Chancellor of the Exchequer (1533), Vicar general (1535), Knight of the Garter (1537), Lord great Chamberlain (1539) and Earl of Essex (1540). His intent to sever all relations with Rome made him many enemies and led to his undoing. He was executed for high treason on 28th July 1540.

EDWARD VI (1537–53) The son of Henry VIII and Jane Seymour. King of England (1547–1553). Under Edward the Reformation begun by Henry gathered momentum and England truly became a Protestant nation.

ELIZABETH I (1533–1603). The daughter of Henry VIII and Anne Boleyn. Queen of England (1558–1603). After Mary's death she restored the protestant Church of England. Under Elizabeth England became a great nation able to withstand the might of Spain, the Armada being defeated in 1588. She never married.

FISHER, JOHN (1469–1535). Scholarly and saintly man. He was a champion of the new learning. Educated at Cambridge and spent much of his life there. He became the first Lady Margaret Professor of Divinity. Later he became Bishop of Rochester. In 1527 he spoke out against the divorce between Henry and Catherine of Aragon, and became a fierce champion of Queen Catherine. Having listened to the Holy Nun of Kent, Elizabeth Barton, he was accused of treason. Went with Thomas More to the Tower. Shortly before his death he was made a cardinal. Executed on 22nd June 1535.

FRANCIS I (1494–1547). Became King of France on 1st January 1515. For much of his reign he was preoccupied with wars with the Emperor. These wars began after Francis had failed to be elected Emperor in 1519. In 1525 the French were routed by the Empire's troops at Pavia. Francis was taken prisoner. He was set free one year later.

MARY (1516–58). Eldest daughter of Henry VIII and Queen of England (1553–58). After her mother, Catherine of Aragon, was divorced, for much of her childhood she lived in constant fear and under the stigma of being illegitimate. She adhered to the Catholic faith and when she became Queen she determined to make England a Catholic country again. To help her in this scheme she married Philip of Spain in 1557. To try to force people to become Catholic many people were burnt, thus earning her the nick name of "Bloody Mary".

MORE, SIR THOMAS (1478–1535). Educated at Oxford, he later became a lawyer. Held several minor posts including Master of Requests (1514), Treasurer of the Exchequer (1521) and Chancellor of the Duchy of Lancaster (1525). On the fall of Wolsey in 1529 he became Lord Chancellor. Although he wished to reform the Church he saw no need to destroy it. He viewed with alarm the successive steps Henry took which led to the break with Rome. He resigned the Chancellorship (1532) and when he refused to swear to the act that made Henry the supreme head of the Church rather than the Pope he was executed (1535).

WOLSEY, THOMAS (c. 1476–1530). Born in Ipswich the son of a butcher. Educated at Oxford University. Became almoner to Henry VIII in 1509 and after the successful campaign in France (1513) offices were showered on him including Archbishop of York (1514) and Cardinal and Lord Chancellor (1515). His downfall was brought about by the collapse of his foreign policy which made him a very unpopular figure because of the taxes he imposed, and his failure to secure a divorce for Henry. Arrested on a charge of high treason, he died on his way to London on 29th November 1530.

Table of Dates

- 1491   Henry born at Greenwich.
- 1501   Prince Arthur and Catherine of Aragon married.
- 1502   Prince Arthur died.
- 1509   April 21st, Death of Henry VII.
  June 11th, Henry and Catherine married.
  June 24th, Coronation of Henry and Catherine.
- 1513   English beat the Scots at Flodden and the French at Guingate, the Battle of the Spurs.
- 1517   Martin Luther nailed his "ninety-five theses" on the door at Wittenberg Cathedral.
- 1519   Charles V elected Holy Roman Emperor.
- 1521   Henry VIII wrote the *Assertio Septem Sacramantorum* against Luther; the Pope gave him the title Defender of the Faith.
- 1527   Rome sacked by Charles' troops.
  Henry began to consider divorcing Catherine.
- 1528   Cardinal Campeggio arrived in England to try the divorce case.
- 1529   Wolsey deprived of his offices.
  The Reformation Parliament opened (November).
- 1530   Wolsey died.
- 1531   Convocation of Clergy acknowledged Henry to be Supreme Head of the Church of England.
- 1532   Submission of the Clergy.
  Sir Thomas More resigned the Lord Chancellorship.
- 1533   Henry secretly married Anne Boleyn (January).
  Cranmer declares Henry's marriage with Catherine invalid and his marriage with Anne to be legal.
  Princess Elizabeth born in September.

1534 Act of Supremacy.
   Act of Succession settled the throne on the heirs by Henry's marriage with Anne Boleyn.
1535 Sir Thomas More and Cardinal Fisher executed.
   Cromwell made Vicar-General in ecclesiastical affairs.
1536 Catherine of Aragon died.
   Monasteries with less than £200 income dissolved.
   Henry VIII's Ten Articles.
   Pilgrimage of Grace in Northern Counties.
   Anne Boleyn executed.
   Henry married Jane Seymour.
1537 Prince Edward born.
   Jane Seymour died.
1538 The Great Bible published in English.
1539 The Six Articles of Religion enacted by Parliament.
   All remaining monasteries dissolved.
1540 Henry married Anne of Cleves and later divorced from her.
   Thomas Cromwell beheaded.
   Henry married Catherine Howard.
1542 Catherine Howard was executed for immorality.
   War with Scotland and Battle of Solway Moss in November.
   James V died and Mary Queen of Scots born.
1543 Henry married Catherine Parr, who survived him.
   Henry allied with Charles V against Francis I.
1544 Boulogne surrendered.
   Sale of monastic land to pay for war with France and debasement of the coinage.
1545 Invasion scare.
1546 Peace made with France.
1547 Henry VIII died, aged 57, at Westminster.

Index

Act of Succession (1534) 54
Act of Succession (1536) 58
Act of Supremacy 54
Anne of Cleves 70–71
Arthur, Prince 8
Aske, Robert 62–63

Barton, Elizabeth (Holy Maid of Kent) 51–52
Battle of the Spurs 19
Beaufort, Elizabeth 36, 40
Blount, Elizabeth 36, 40
Boleyn, Anne 40, 48–51, 55, 57–58
Bosworth, Battle of 7
Boulogne, Siege of 79

Campeggio, Cardinal Lorenzo 42–44
Catherine of Aragon 9, 36, 42–43, 50, 55
Catholicism 61, 72
Charles V, Holy Roman Emperor 36–39, 44
Clergy, the 46–47
Cranmer, Thomas 49–50, 67, 84
Cromwell, Thomas 53, 59, 67–69, 71–73
Council, the 11, 16, 17
Court banquets and entertainments 9, 13, 65
Coverdale's Bible 66–67
Culpepper, Thomas 75–76

Debasement of the coinage 82
Defense of the Seven Sacraments 34
Dereham, Francis 75–76
Dissolution of the Monasteries 59–60

Edward, Prince 58, 76, 82
Elizabeth, Princess 51, 76
Erasmus, Desiderius 31

Ferdinand I, King of Spain 16–18

Fisher, John, Bishop of Rochester 43, 52
Flodden, Battle of 19–20
Fox, Richard, Bishop of Winchester 11
Francis I, King of France 25, 27, 49, 64, 69, 78

Hampton Court 23–24
Henry VII, King of England 7, 8, 23–24
Henry VIII, King of England
—birth 8
—coronation 9
—education 30
—appearance 8, 45, 74–75
—extravagance 15
—interest in music 30–31
—relations with Parliament 38, 47–48
—need for money 38, 60, 64, 82
—accidents 45–46
—illness 40, 46, 56, 75–76
—attitude to religion 36, 72
—style of government 68
—love of war 78–79
—interest in the Navy 81–82
—death 83–84
—achievement 85–88
Holbein, Hans 66, 70
Holy League of Spain 17
Holy Roman Empire 33
Household of Henry VIII 65
Howard, Catherine 72, 74–76
Hunting and hawking 14

Invasion, threat of 69, 80

James IV, King of Scotland 19
James V, King of Scotland 78
Jousting 9, 13, 27

Louis XII, King of France 16, 20

Luther, Martin 33–34

Mary Stuart, Queen of Scots 79
Mary Tudor, Queen of England 20, 25, 35, 44, 62, 76
Maximilian, Emperor 16, 18, 20, 29
More, Sir Thomas 31–32, 48, 52–53

Nonsuch Palace 64
Norfolk, Duke of 63, 72–73, 78
Parr, Catherine 76, 84
Pavia, Battle of 37
Pilgrimage of Grace 62
Pope, the
—Clement VII 37, 42
—Paul III 52, 69
—Julius II 17, 18
Protestantism 42, 61, 67, 69–70, 73

Renaissance, the 31
Richard III, King of England 7
Richmond, Duke of 36
Ruthell, Thomas, Bishop of Durham 11

Saint George's Chapel, Windsor 58, 84
Scotland 78
Seymour, Jane 56, 58
Six Acts, the 72
Solway Moss, Battle of 78
Submission of the clergy 48

Ten Acts, the 61
Theouranne, Siege of 19
Tournai, Siege of 19–20
Tower of London 52, 57, 73

Val d'Or (Field of Cloth of Gold) 27–29

Wareham, William, Archbishop of Canterbury 11, 49
Wolsey, Sir Thomas 21, 23–24, 26–28, 36–39, 44

95

Further Reading

There are many lives of Henry VIII. Among the best are: J. J. Scarisbrick, *Henry VIII* (Pelican, 1971); A. F. Pollard, *Henry VIII* (1905, current edition, Jonathan Cape, 1970); Robert Lacey, *The Life and Times of Henry VIII* (Weidenfeld and Nicolson, 1972); Neville Williams, *Henry VIII and his Court* (Cardinal, 1973). The first two provide scholarly introductions to how two first-rate historians interpret Henry's complex character. The second two are popular, and contain many admirable illustrations, and the fourth gives a good picture of life in Henry's court.

Biographies abound of Henry's principal subjects. A very useful collection of essays, written with accuracy and brevity, can be found in Katherine Garvin (ed.), *The Great Tudors* (1956, now out of print).

For the social and religious background the following may be consulted: G. M. Trevelyan, *Illustrated English Social History: Volume I* (Pelican, 1968); Roger Hart, *English Life in Tudor Times* (Wayland, 1972); T. M. Parker, *The English Reformation to 1558* (Oxford, 1960); A. G. Dickens, *The English Reformation* (Batsford, 1964). The first two are admirably suited for children especially the second with lucid text and plentiful illustrations. The second two books are authoritative accounts of the Reformation. In addition, a useful and carefully edited selection of documents is to be found in *The Reformation*, L. W. Cowie (Wayland, 1970).

Picture Credits

The author and publisher are grateful to the following for their kind permission to reproduce illustrations on the pages shown:
The British Museum, 6, 45, 66; The London Museum, 64; The Mansell Collection, 12, 13, 14, 20, 30, 46, 47, 49, 57, 71, 76, 78; The National Portrait Gallery, 22, 32 (left), 50, 53; The Radio Times Hulton Picture Library, *frontispiece*, 12, 20, 23, 41, 61, 80; the remaining pictures are the property of the Wayland Picture Library.

92 Fletcher
H
    HENRY VIII

19930

92 Fletcher
H
    HENRY VIII

19930

MAR 21 '84	864		
NOV 3 '86	405		
APR 3 '92	720		

Fort Edward Free Library
23 East Street
Fort Edward, N.Y. 12828

FORT EDWARD FREE LIBRARY - NY
0 00 27 0007128 1